Patient Love Is Kind

Coloring With Kindness

Patient Love Is Kind

We live in a world where being patient is not magnified and being Kind is considered weak. Love allows us to color in the blurred lines through Kindness

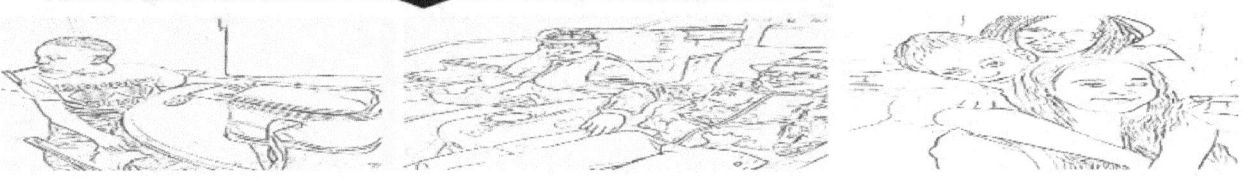

COLORING WITH KINDNESS
#THISISTHEKINDNESS

Patient Love Is Kind
Richard Patterson III

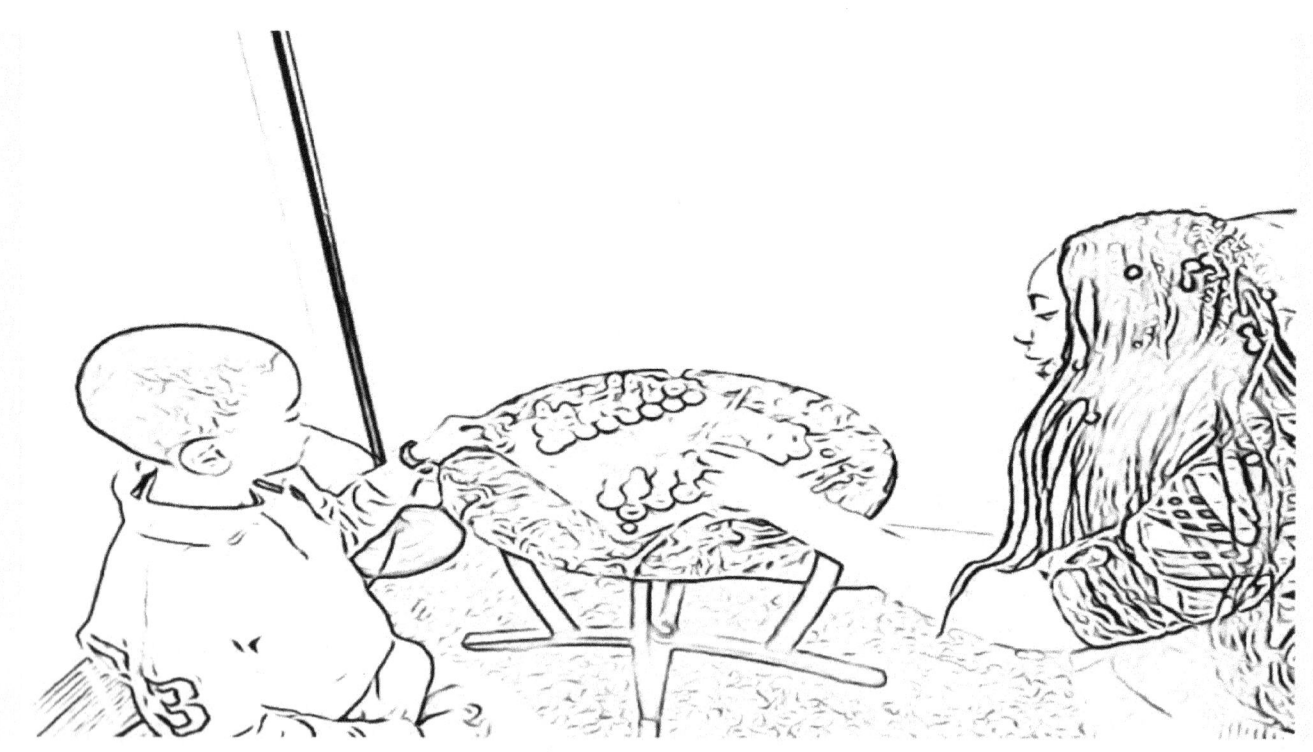

Life like chess requires patience in order to make the right moves to advance.

Coloring With Kindness, Page 2

Patient Love Is Kind
Richard Patterson III

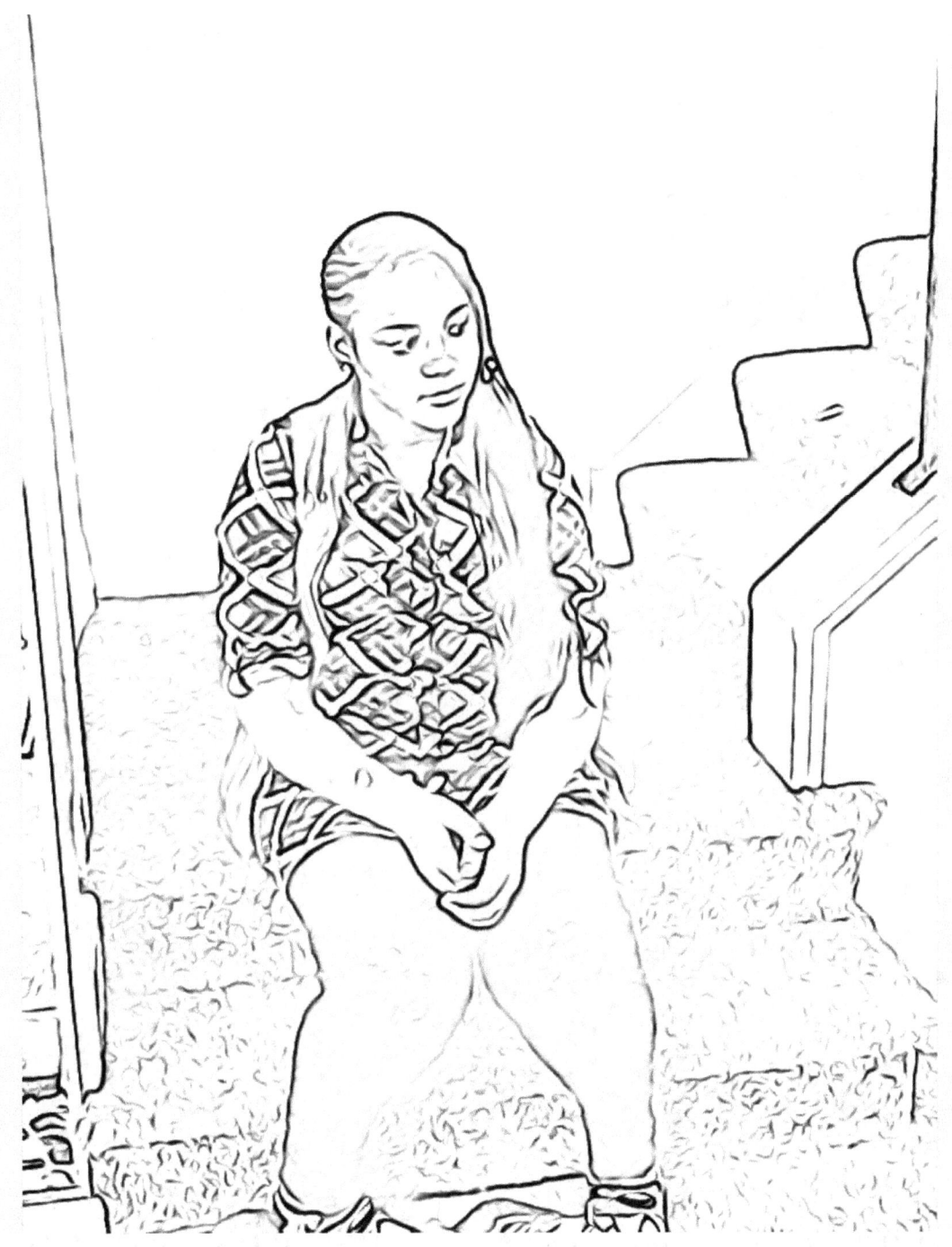

What you focus on cultivates your ability to be patient. Children need a direction in order to develop their patience.

Coloring With Kindness, Page 3

Patient Love Is Kind
Richard Patterson III

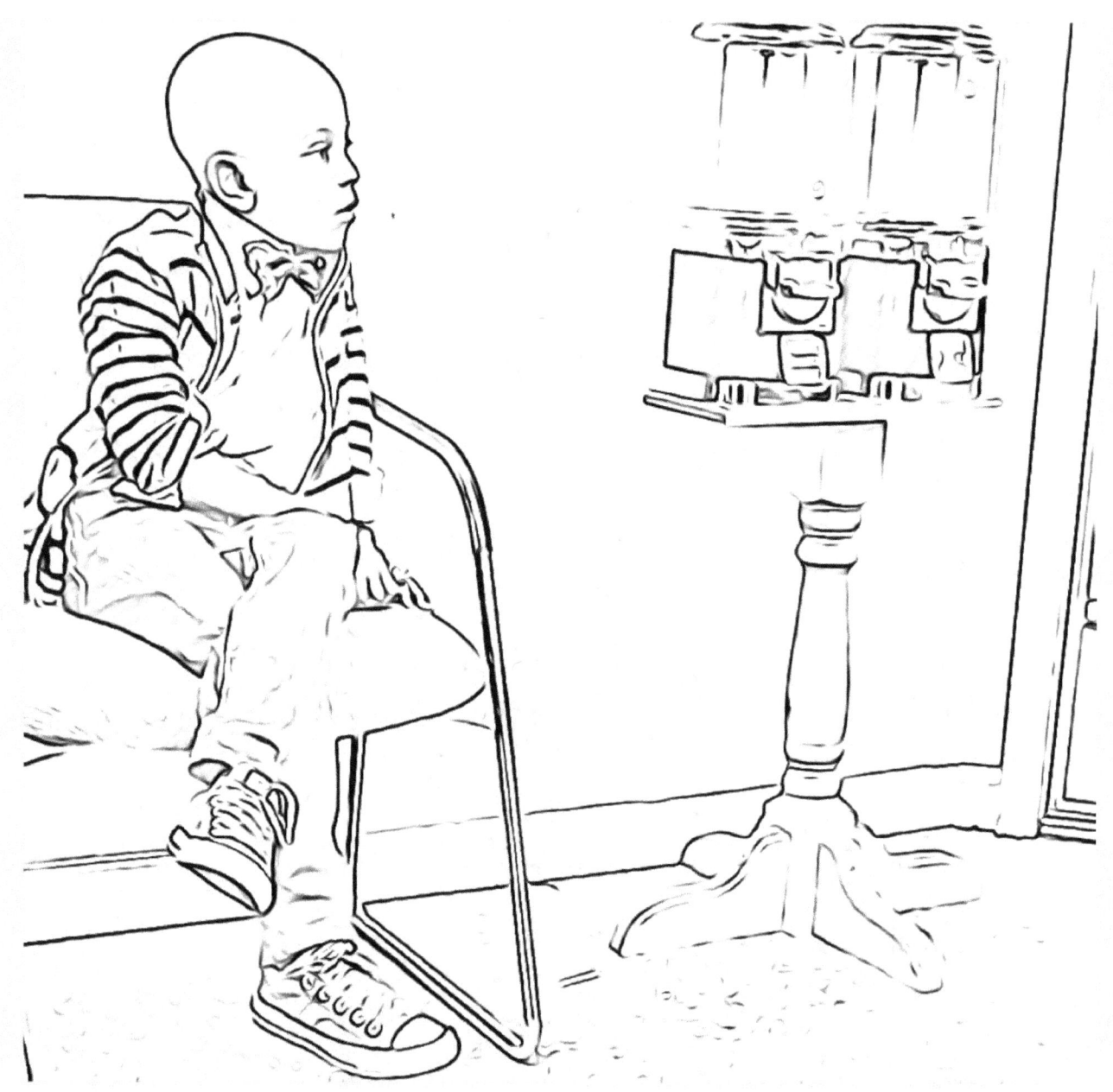

Sometimes being left alone with your thoughts leaves space for you to be creative. Patience cultivates the creativity in our children.

Patient Love Is Kind
Richard Patterson III

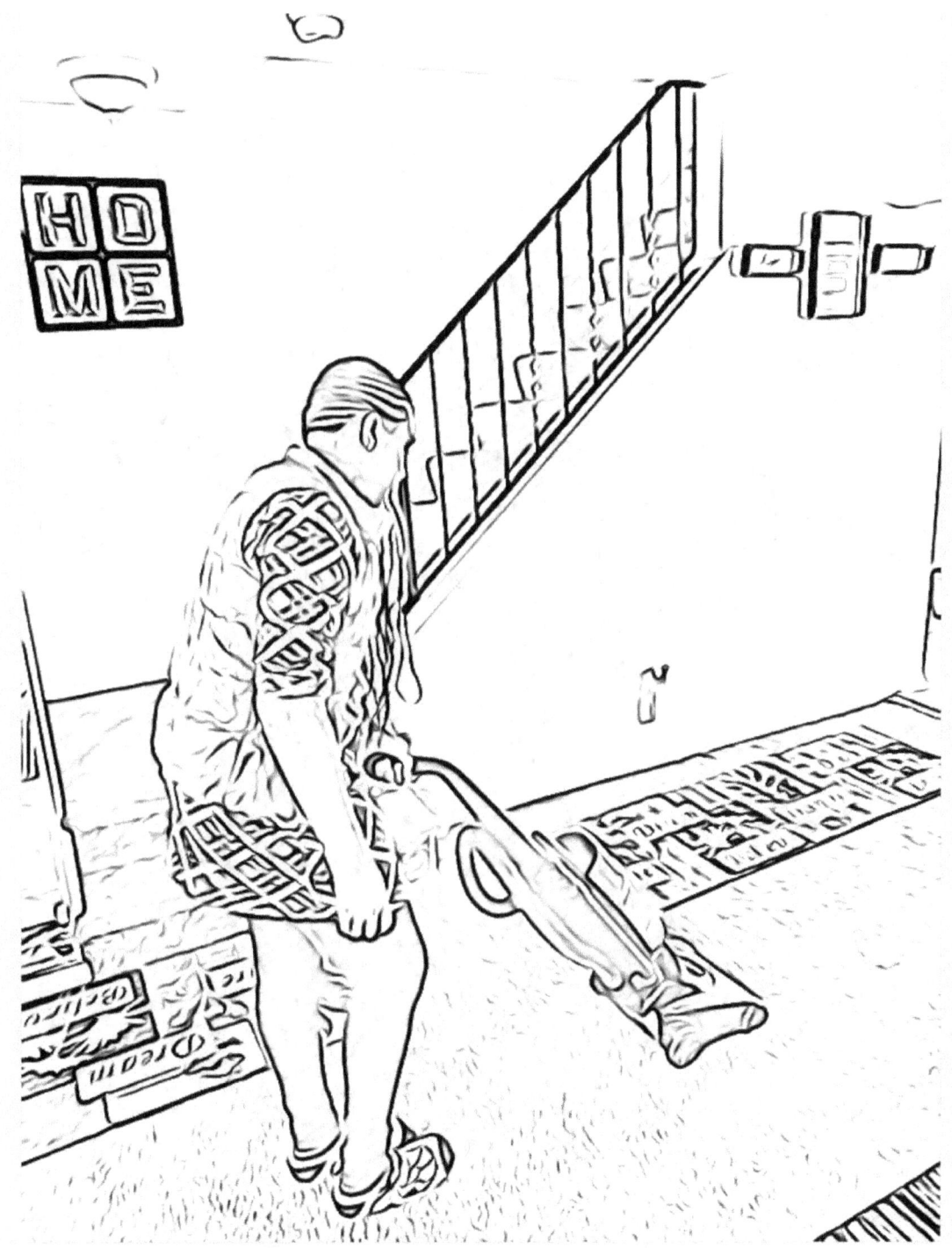

Patience like a vacuum focuses on one particular area and moves on as directed. Children learn patience the same way as they are directed.

Patient Love Is Kind
Richard Patterson III

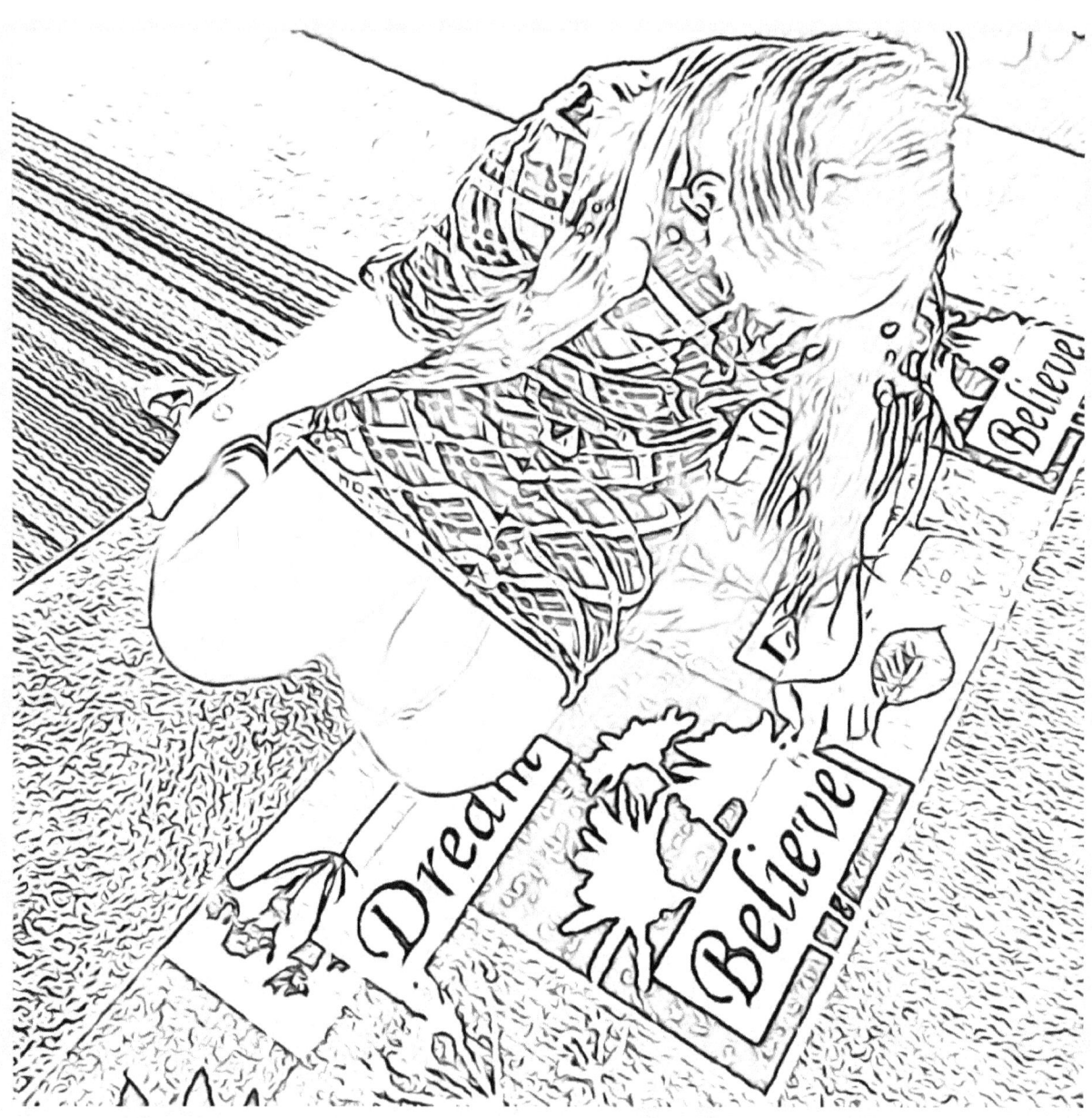

Patience allows you to see the things that are right under your nose. Patient children have the creativity to believe and dream.

Coloring With Kindness, Page 6

Patient Love Is Kind
Richard Patterson III

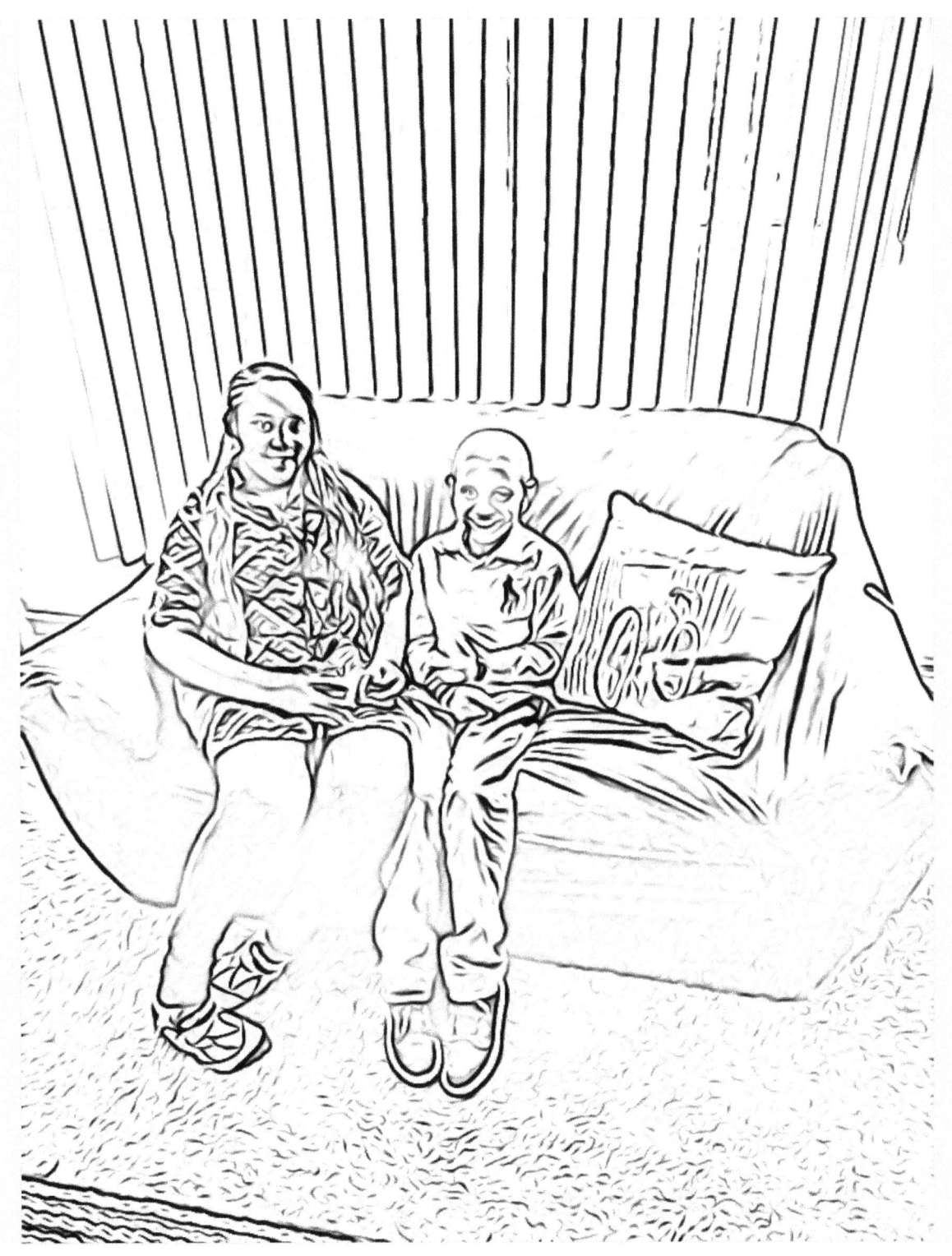

On a loveseat two people need a spot, it's the same way with children. They learn to co-exist while space is being shared. Developing their patience

Patient Love Is Kind
Richard Patterson III

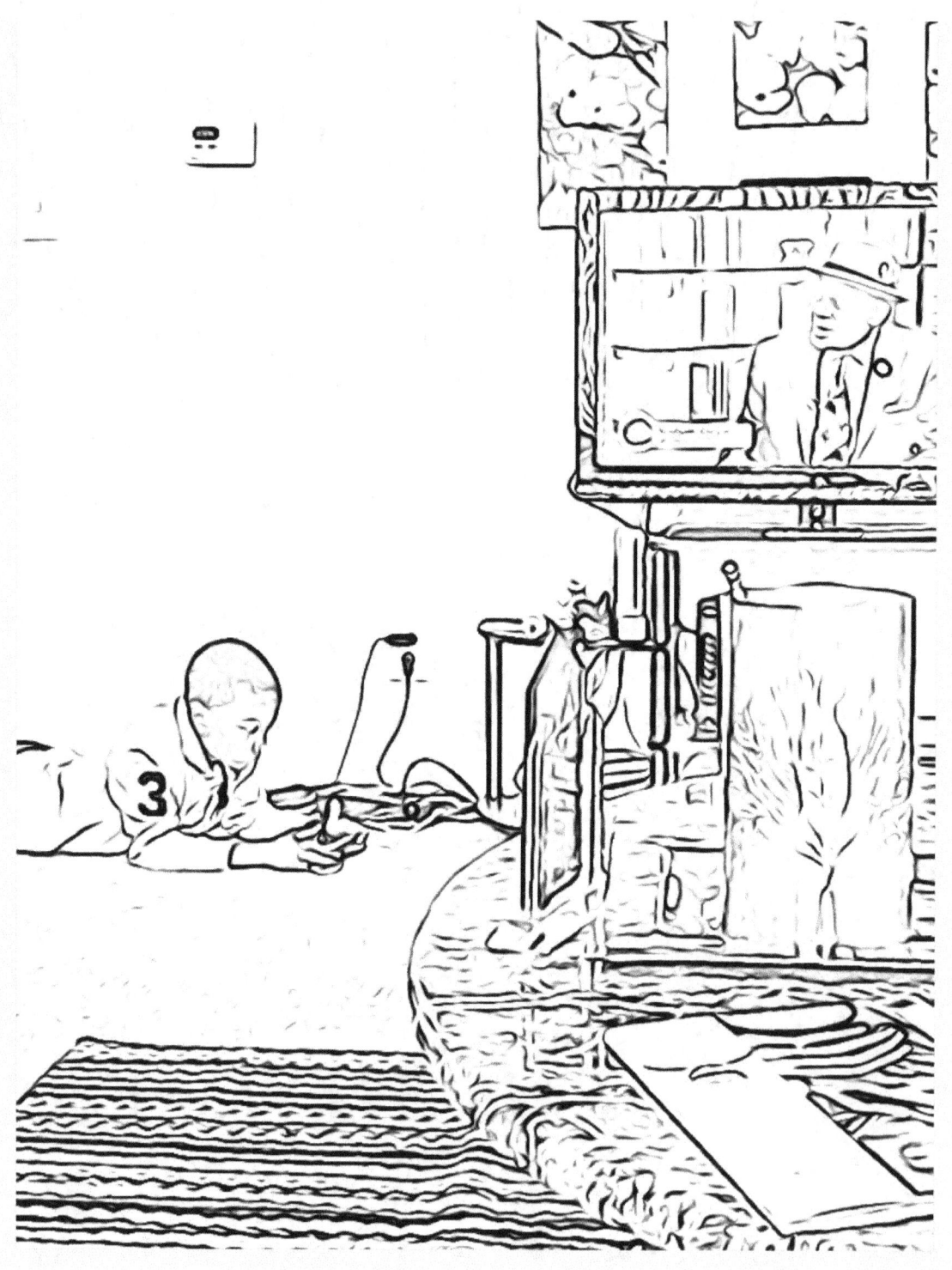

Sometimes the best recreation is staying at the house and learning to enjoy your home environment. Patience has a lot to do with the pace we live our lives.

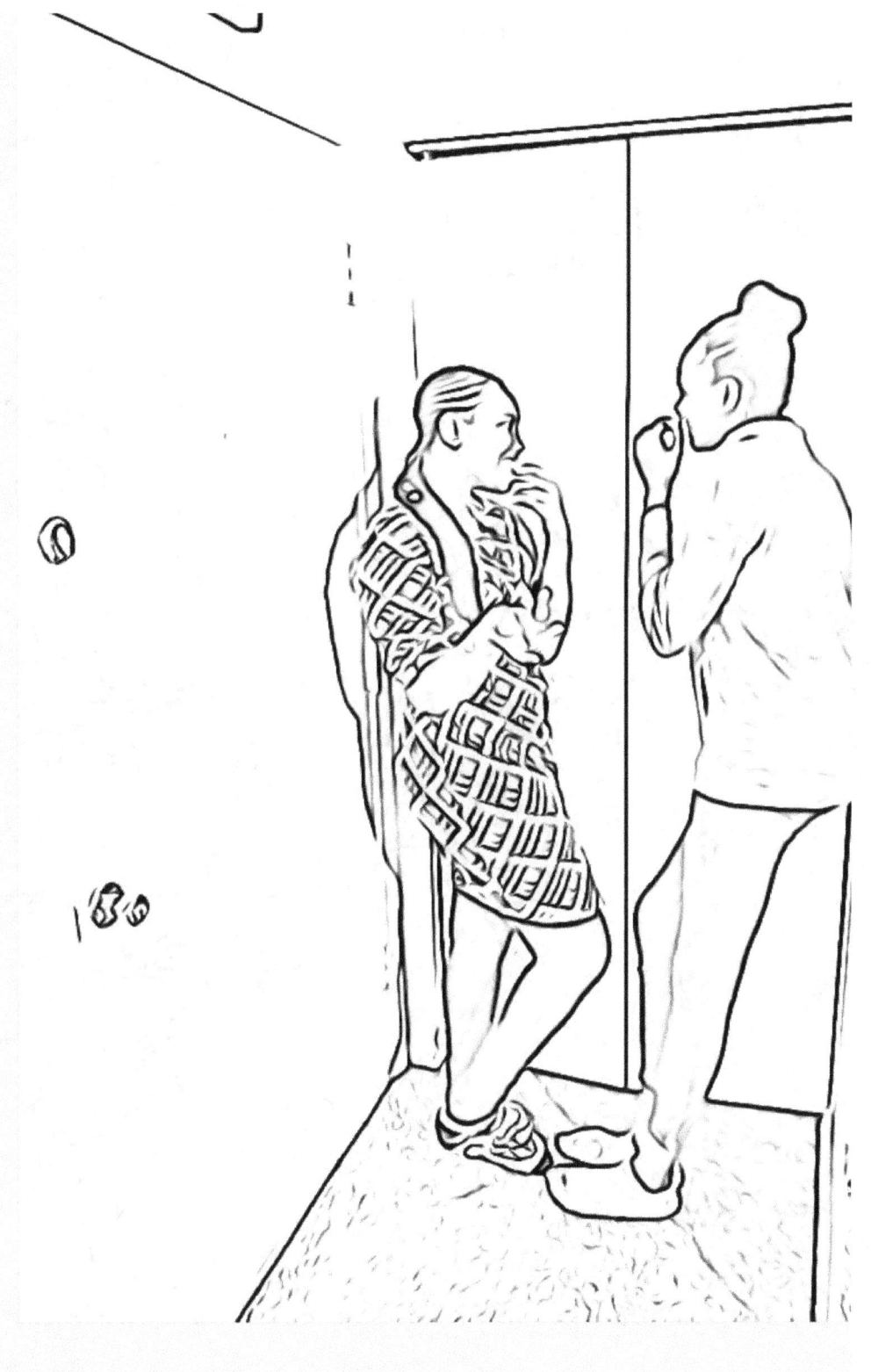

Patience helps you to create good moments right where you are.

Patient Love Is Kind
Richard Patterson III

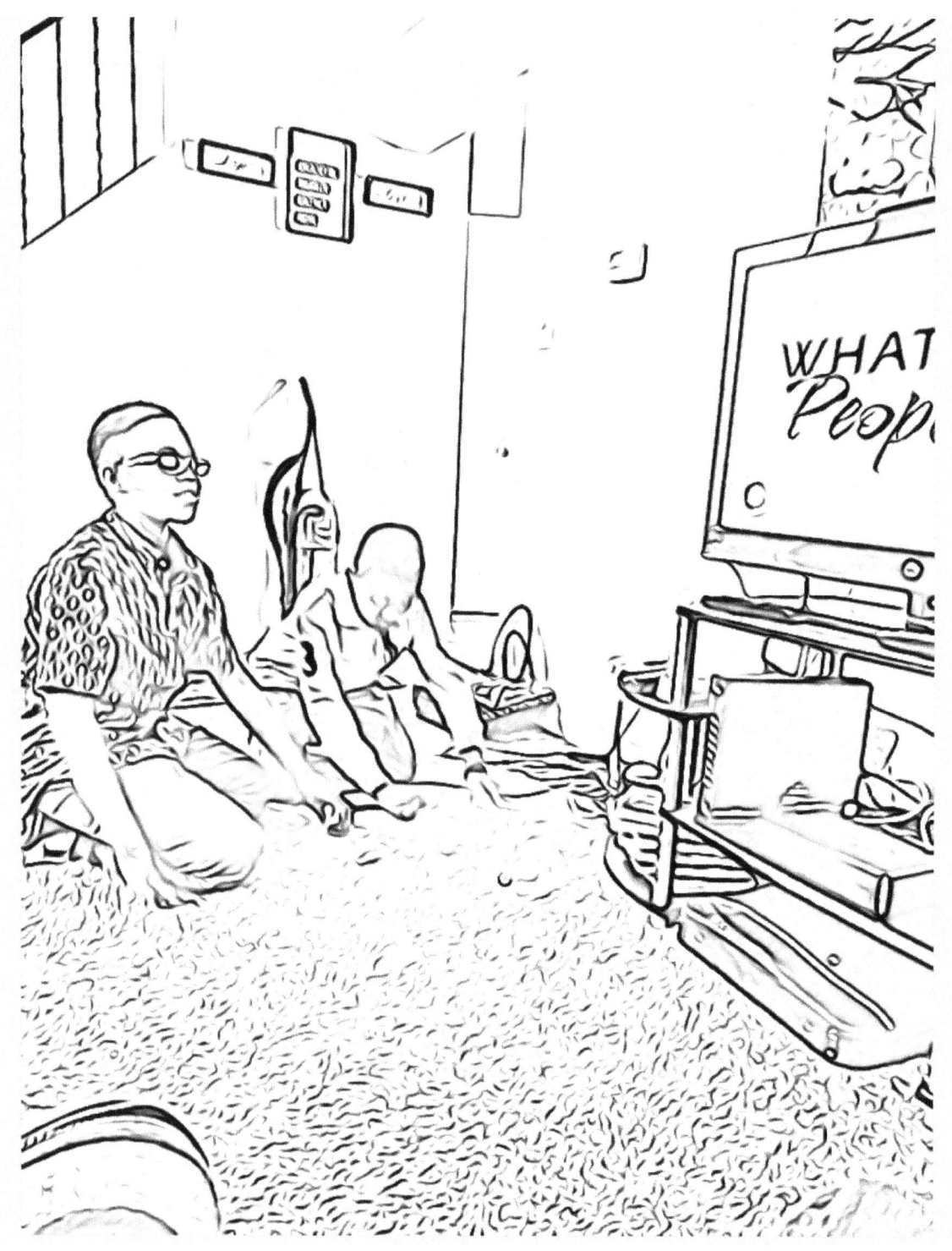

Patience is all about "US" what serves both parties. I may not be into what you're into but I'm open to you enjoying this moment.

Coloring With Kindness, Page 10

Patient Love Is Kind
Richard Patterson III

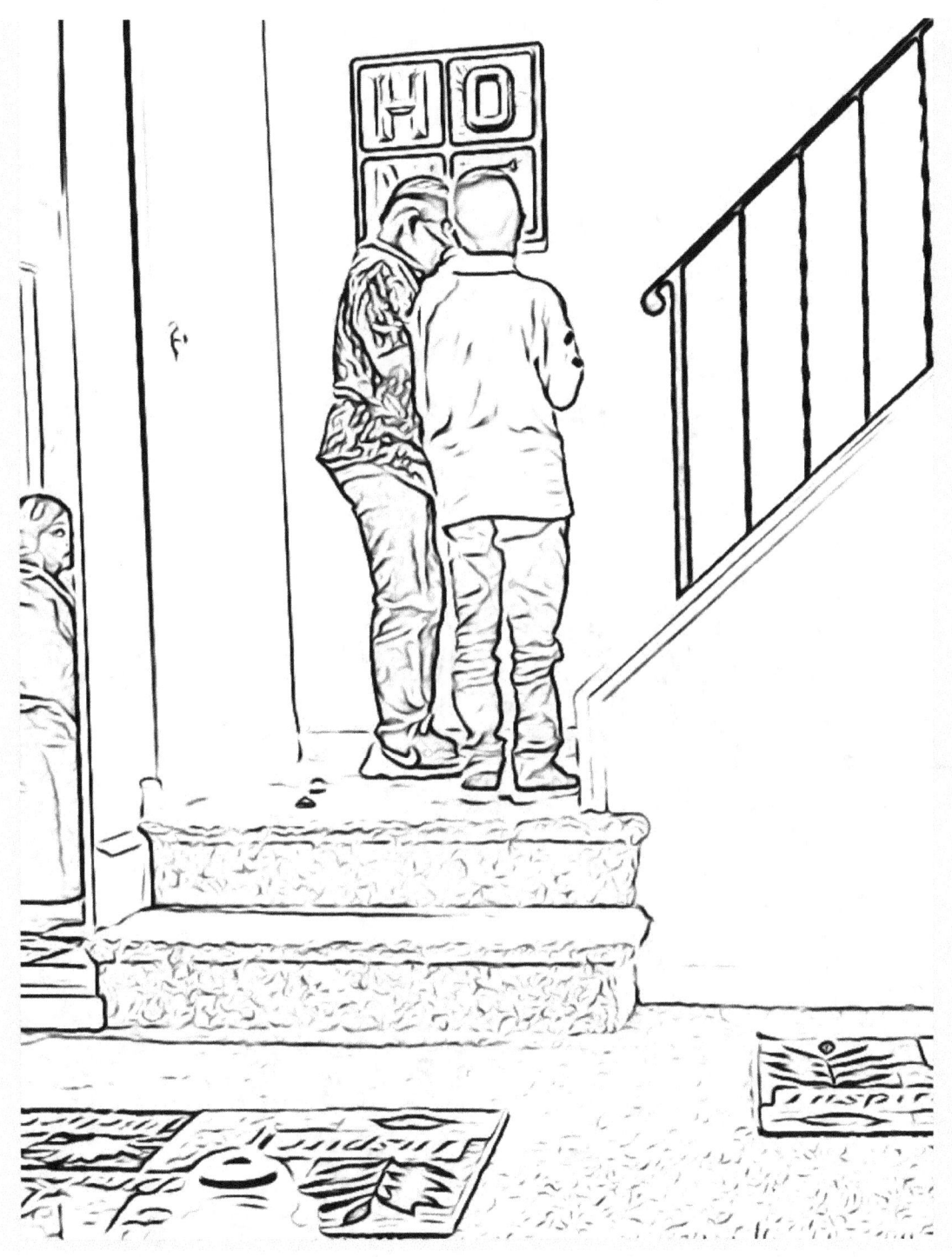

Patience understands life will allow the next moment to be about me. Children learn patience by understanding the value of seeing beyond this moment.

Patient Love Is Kind
Richard Patterson III

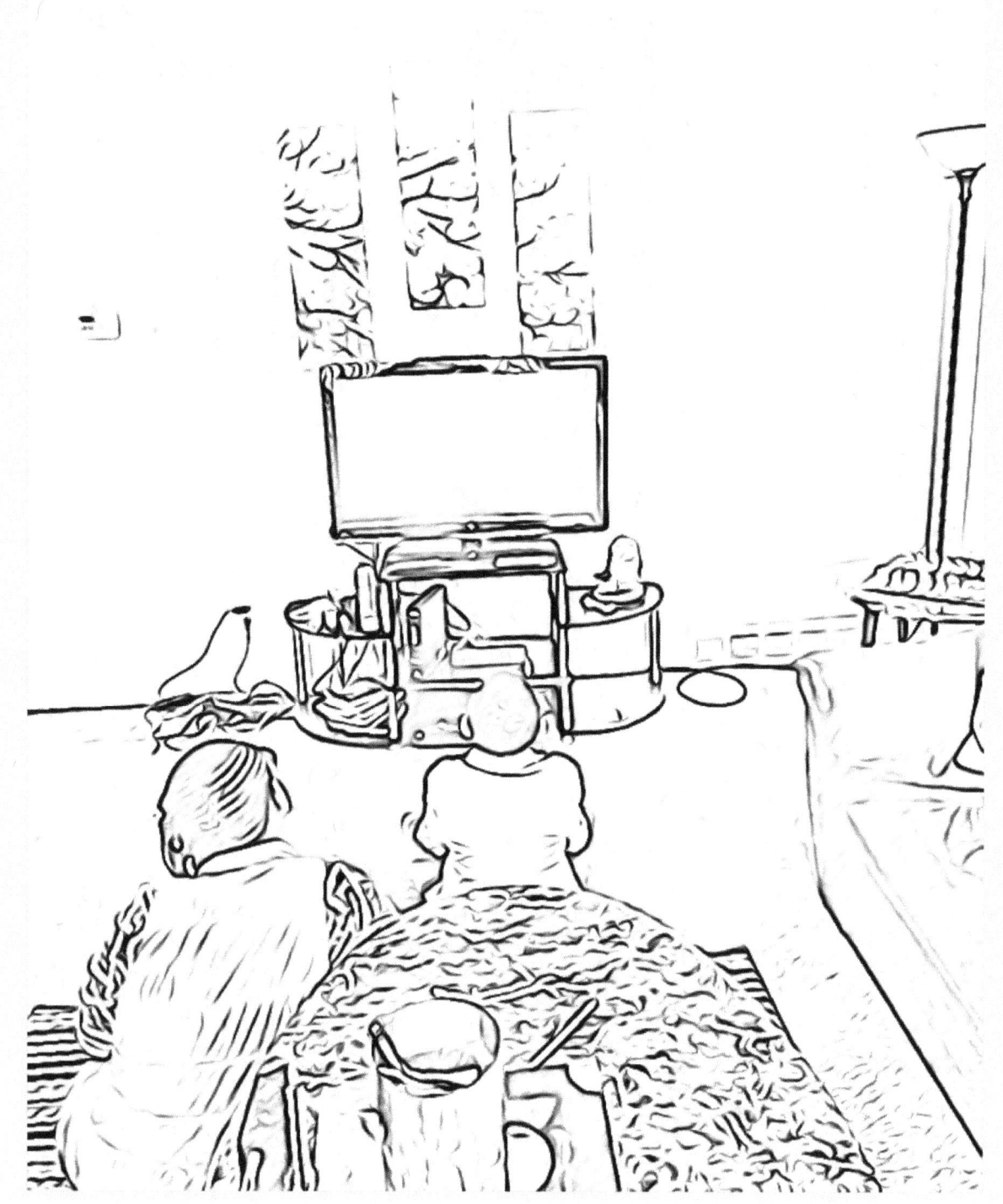

Patience grows over time allowing concessions to be made. Children learn to see outside of themselves as they are positioned to share in environments.

Patient Love Is Kind
Richard Patterson III

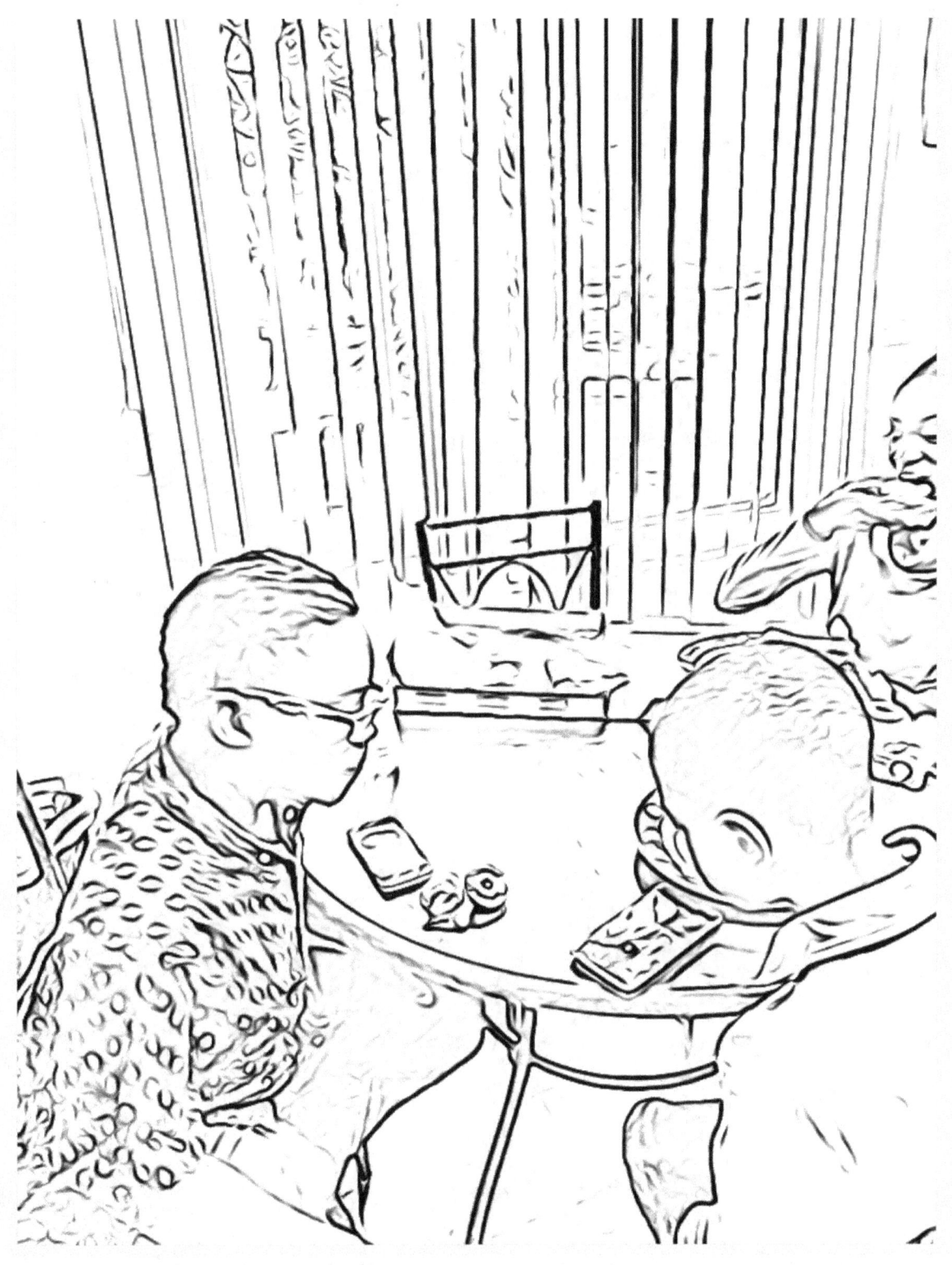

Kindness is being interested enough to care about what the other person values.

Coloring With Kindness, Page 13

Patient Love Is Kind
Richard Patterson III

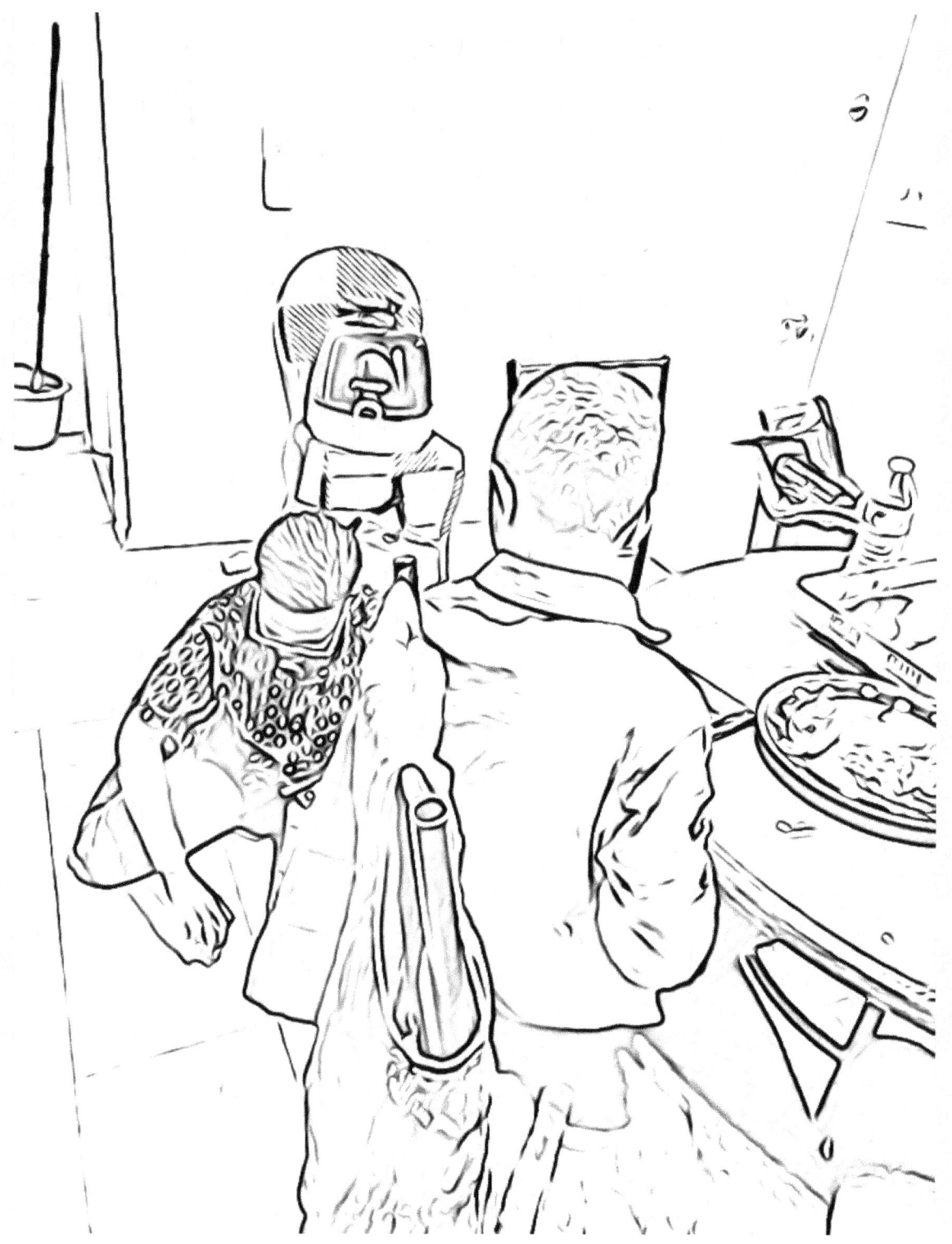

Children will find a way to play, and Kindness is the same way. Agreeable and easy going about life.

Coloring With Kindness, Page 14

Patient Love Is Kind
Richard Patterson III

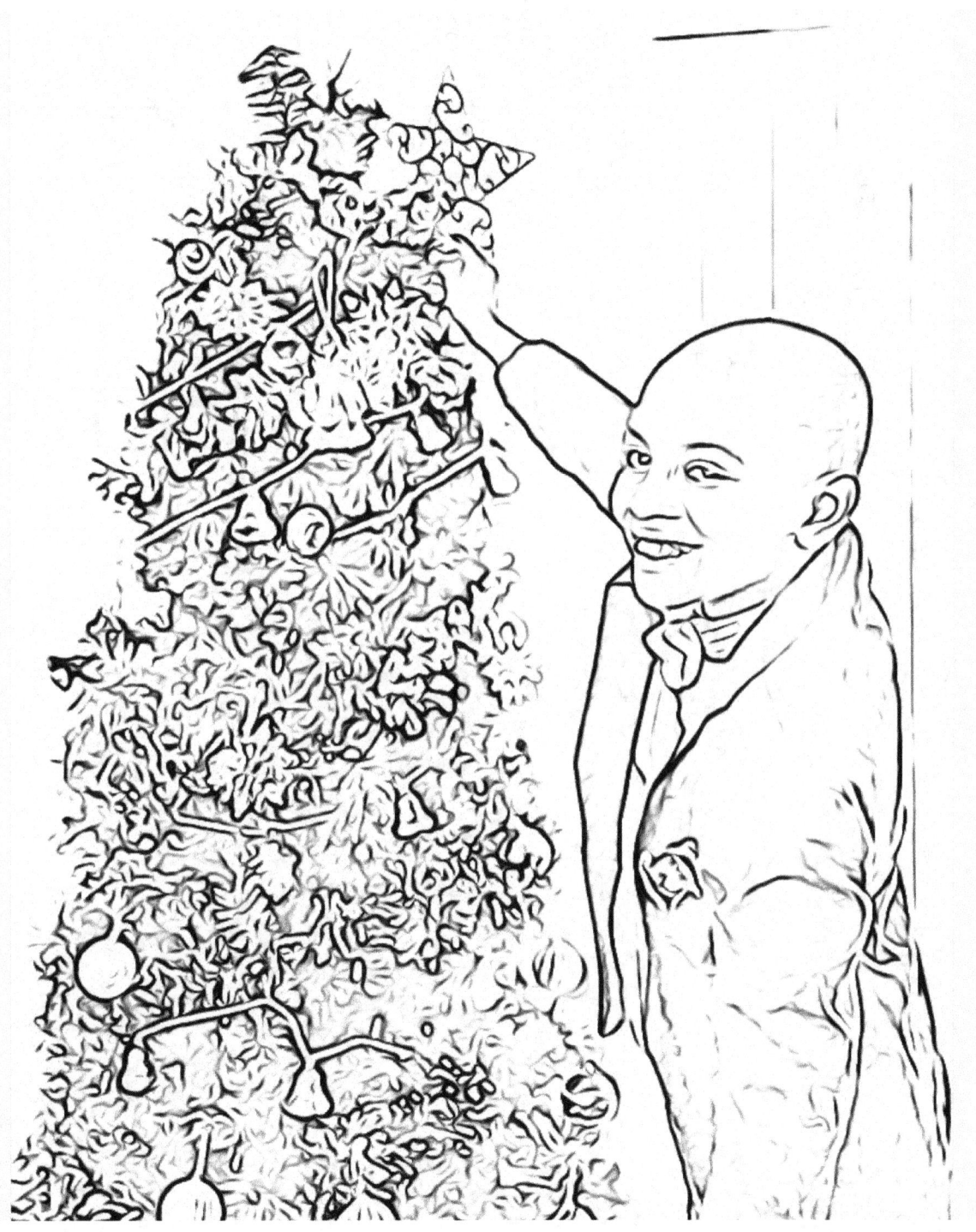

Like an ornament on a tree Kindness will stand out in any room.

Coloring With Kindness, Page 15

Patient Love Is Kind
Richard Patterson III

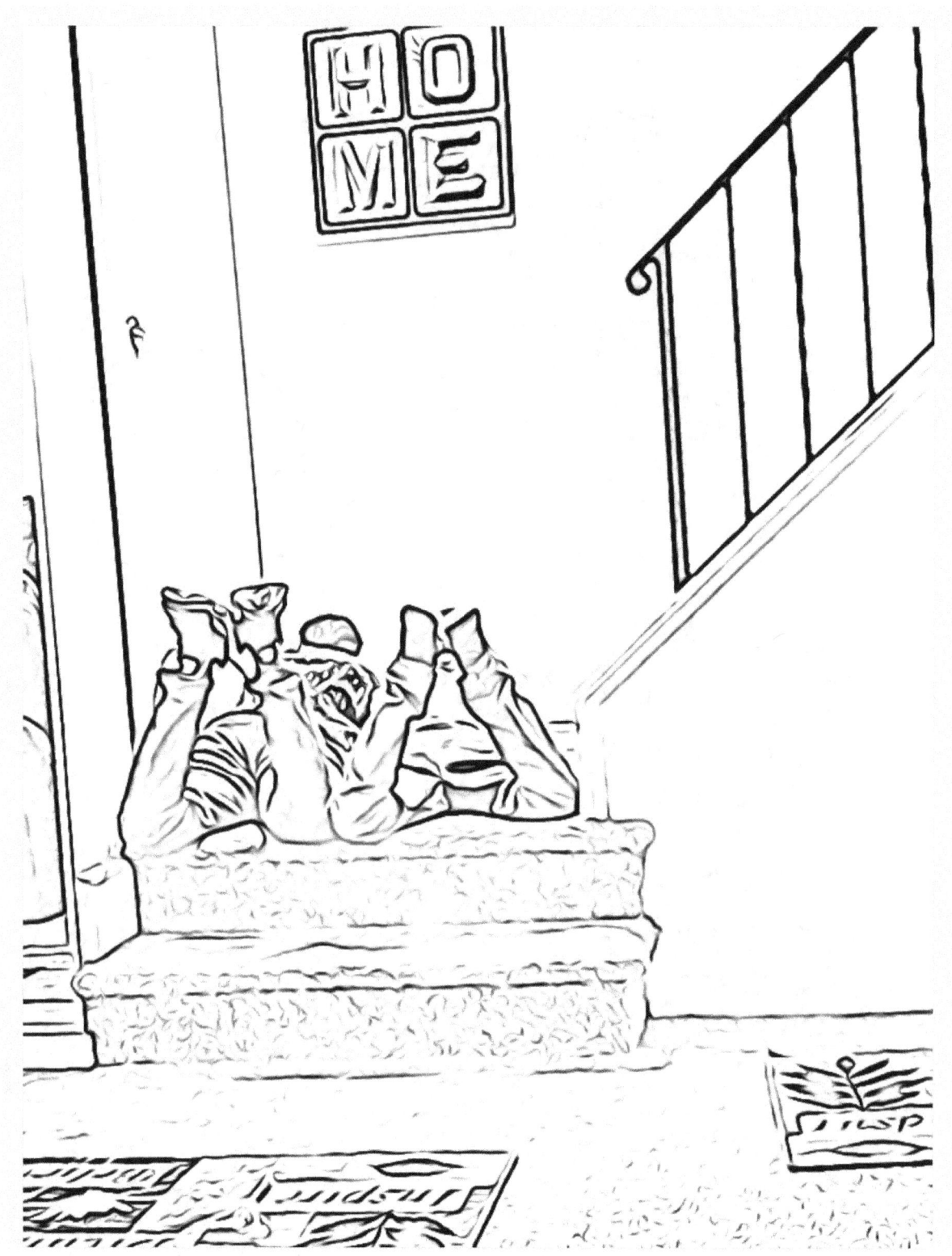

Kindness will find a way to be in the room.
Creating beautiful moments for others

Coloring With Kindness, Page 16

Patient Love Is Kind
Richard Patterson III

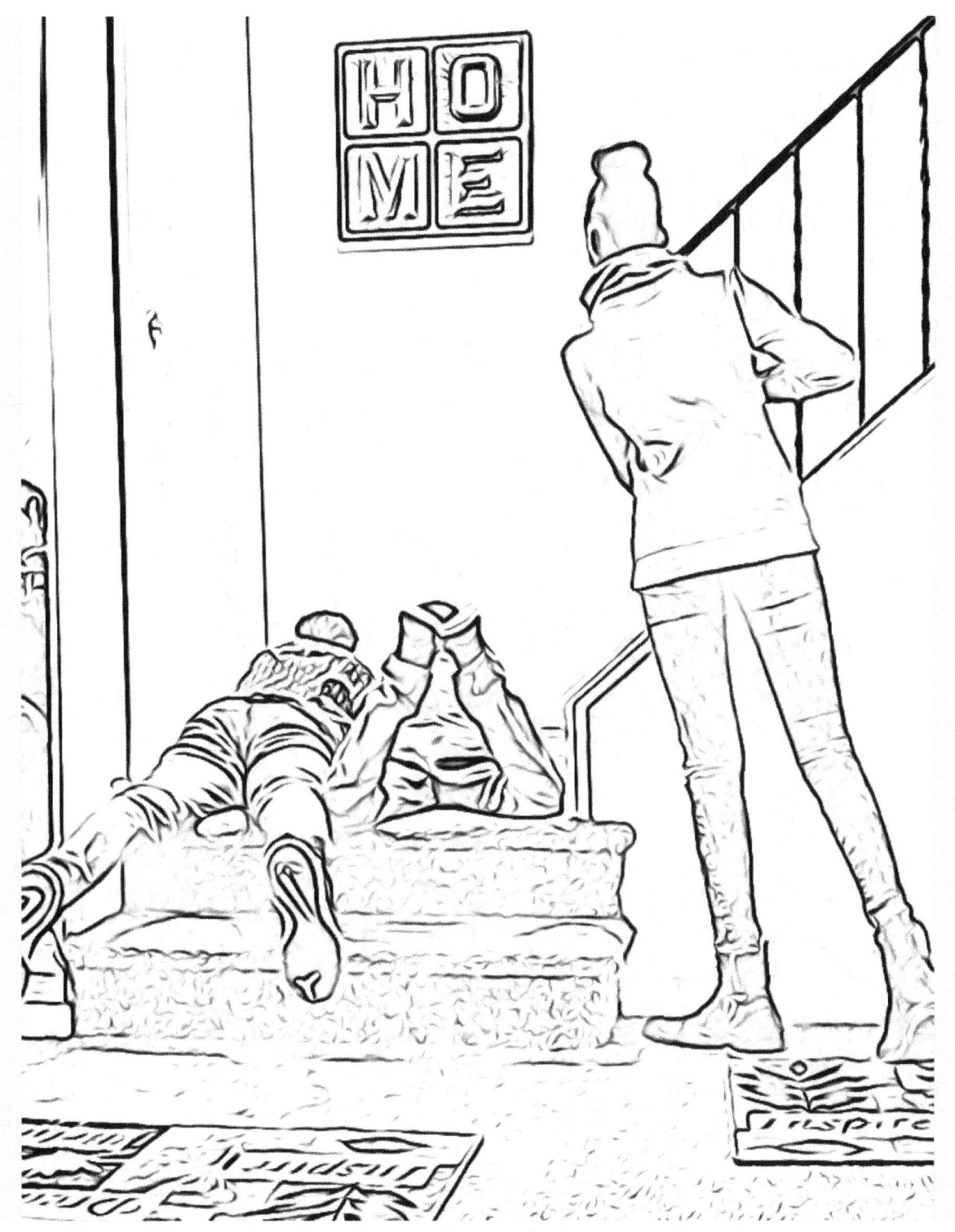

Kindness makes others inquisitive about what's so good. Kindness cultivates the good in all of us

Patient Love Is Kind
Richard Patterson III

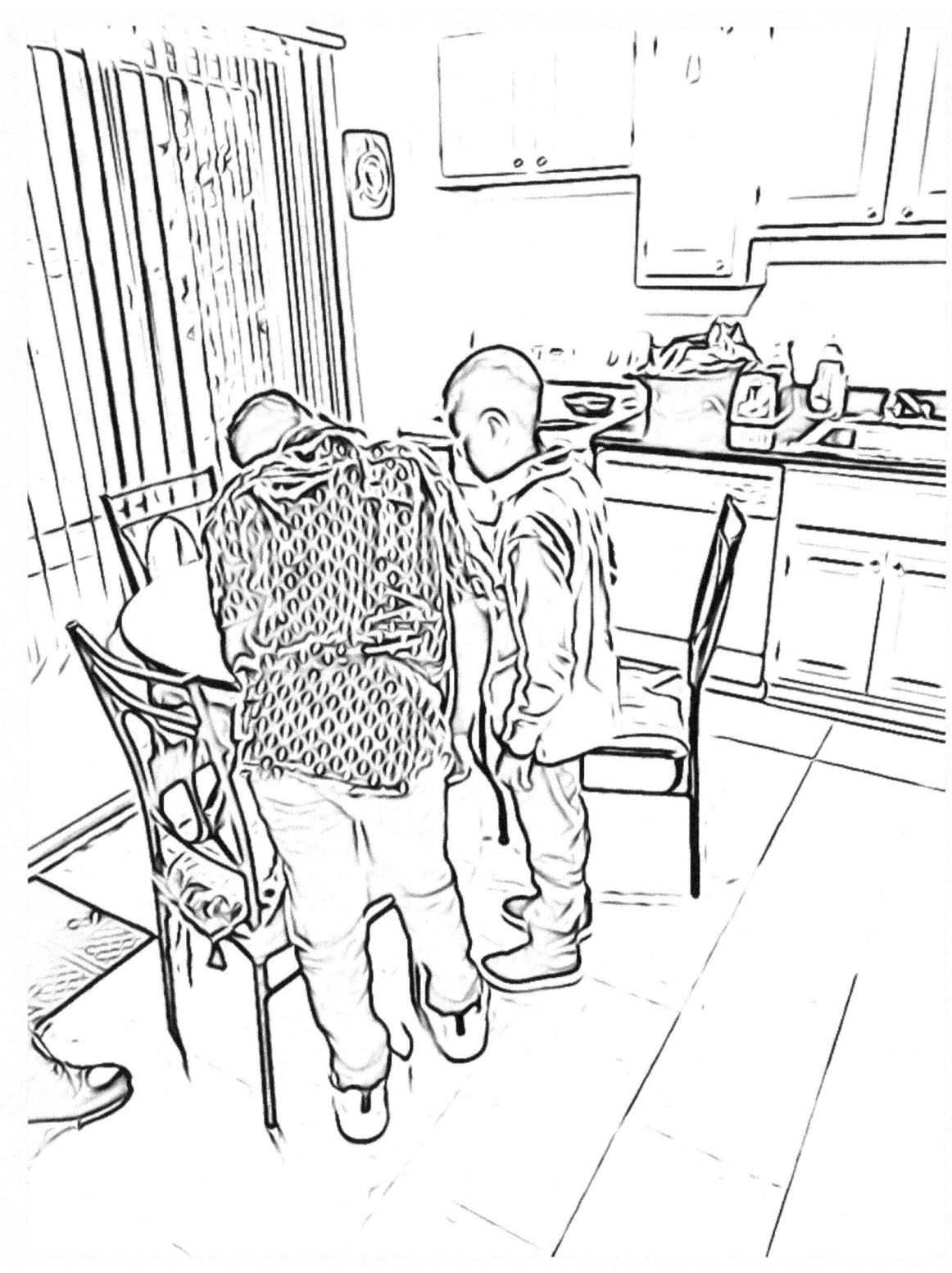

Kindness impacts the space you live in positively. Children make the world a place where Kindness resides.

Patient Love Is Kind
Richard Patterson III

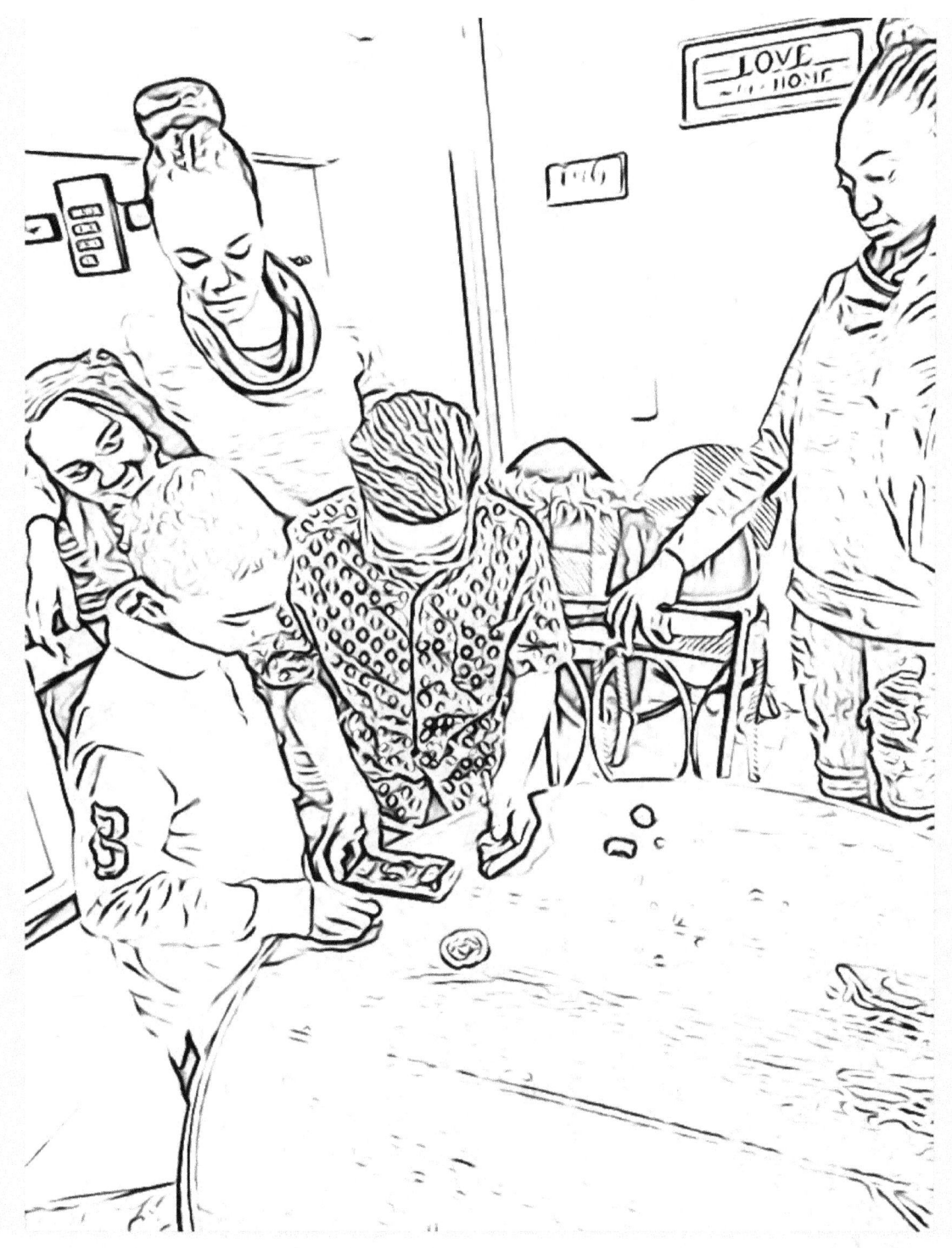

Kindness grows the positivity in the environment, because your genuine interest in others is contagious. Children are the positive carriers of Kindness.

Coloring With Kindness, Page 19

Patient Love Is Kind
Richard Patterson III

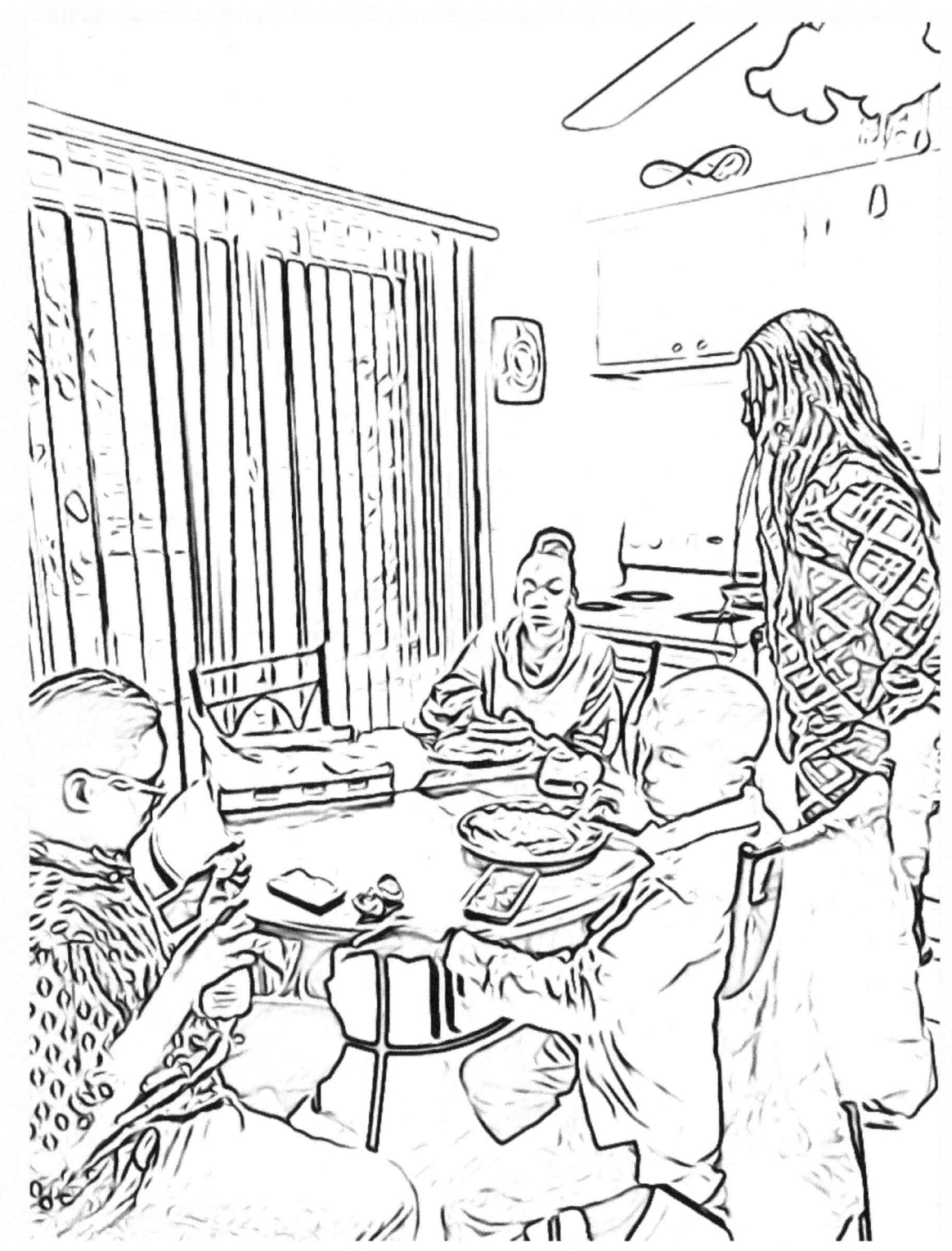

Like a table Kindness is welcoming, willing to stay for the demands that may be placed on it.

Patient Love Is Kind
Richard Patterson III

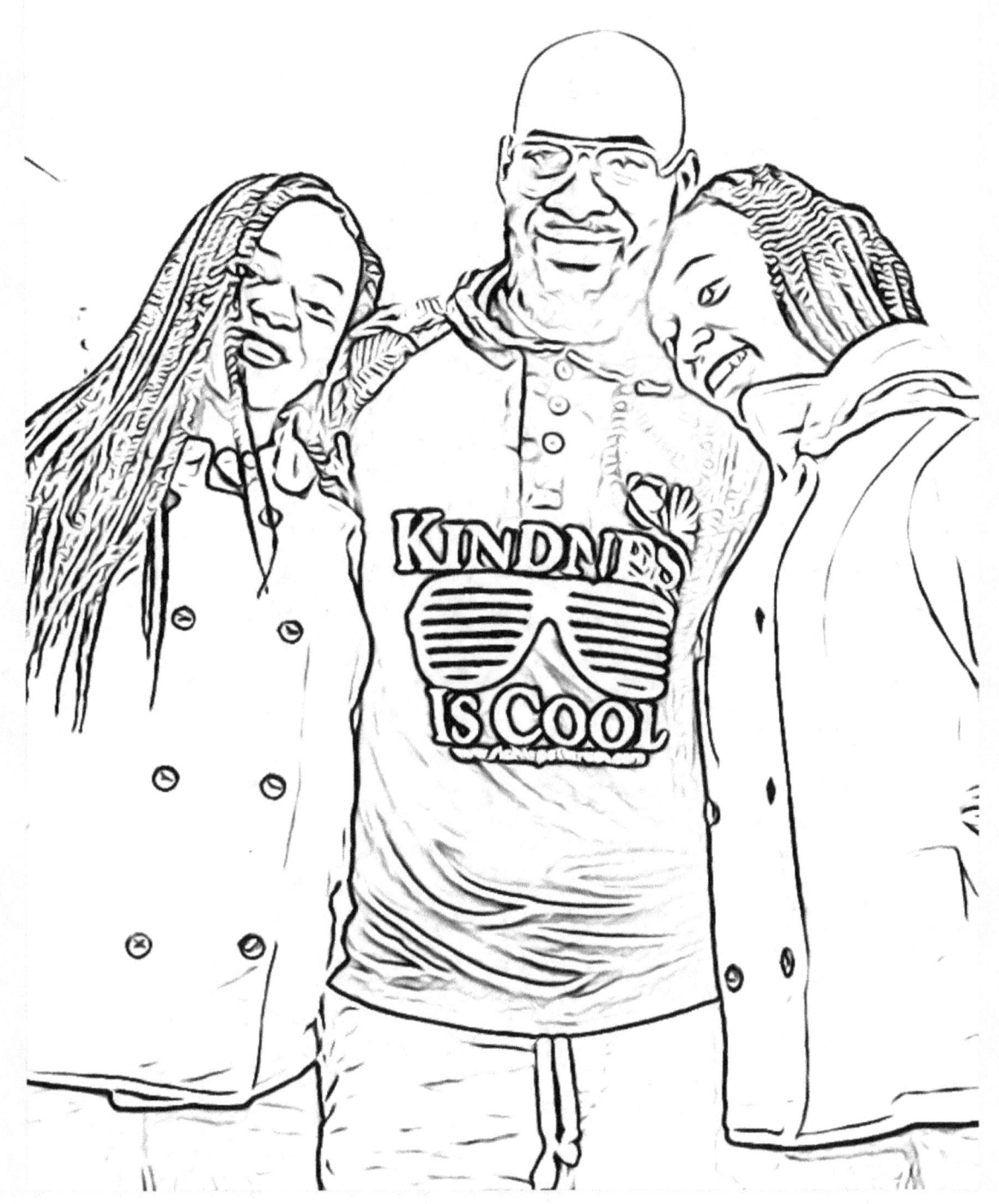

Love is the greatest force in the earth and gives us a purpose. Children were made to deposit that love into.

Patient Love Is Kind
Richard Patterson III

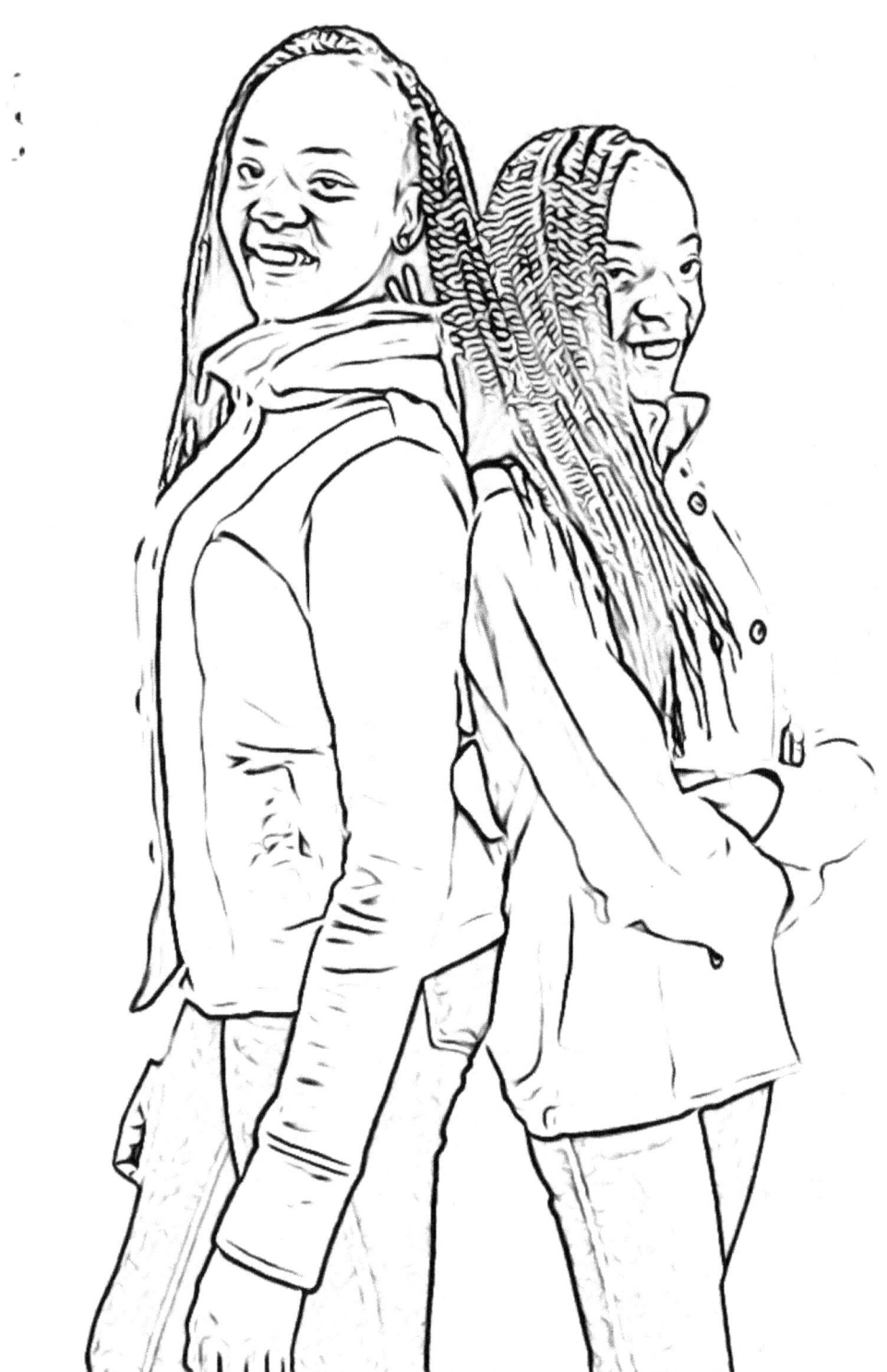

Love is a decision to embrace every facet of a person.

Coloring With Kindness, Page 22

Patient Love Is Kind
Richard Patterson III

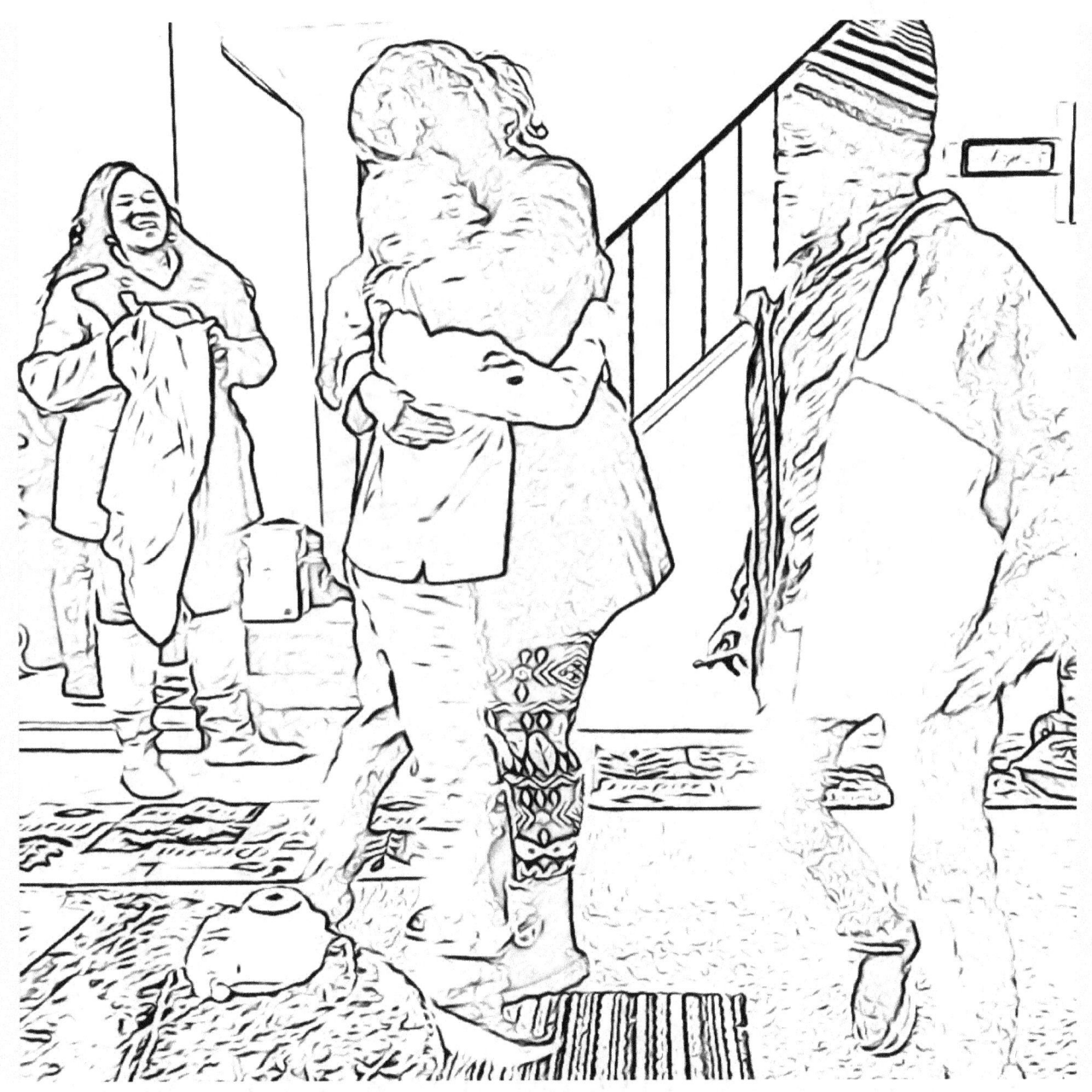

Even when love is not being expressed to you.
Love is just happy to see that someone else
benefits from it.

Patient Love Is Kind
Richard Patterson III

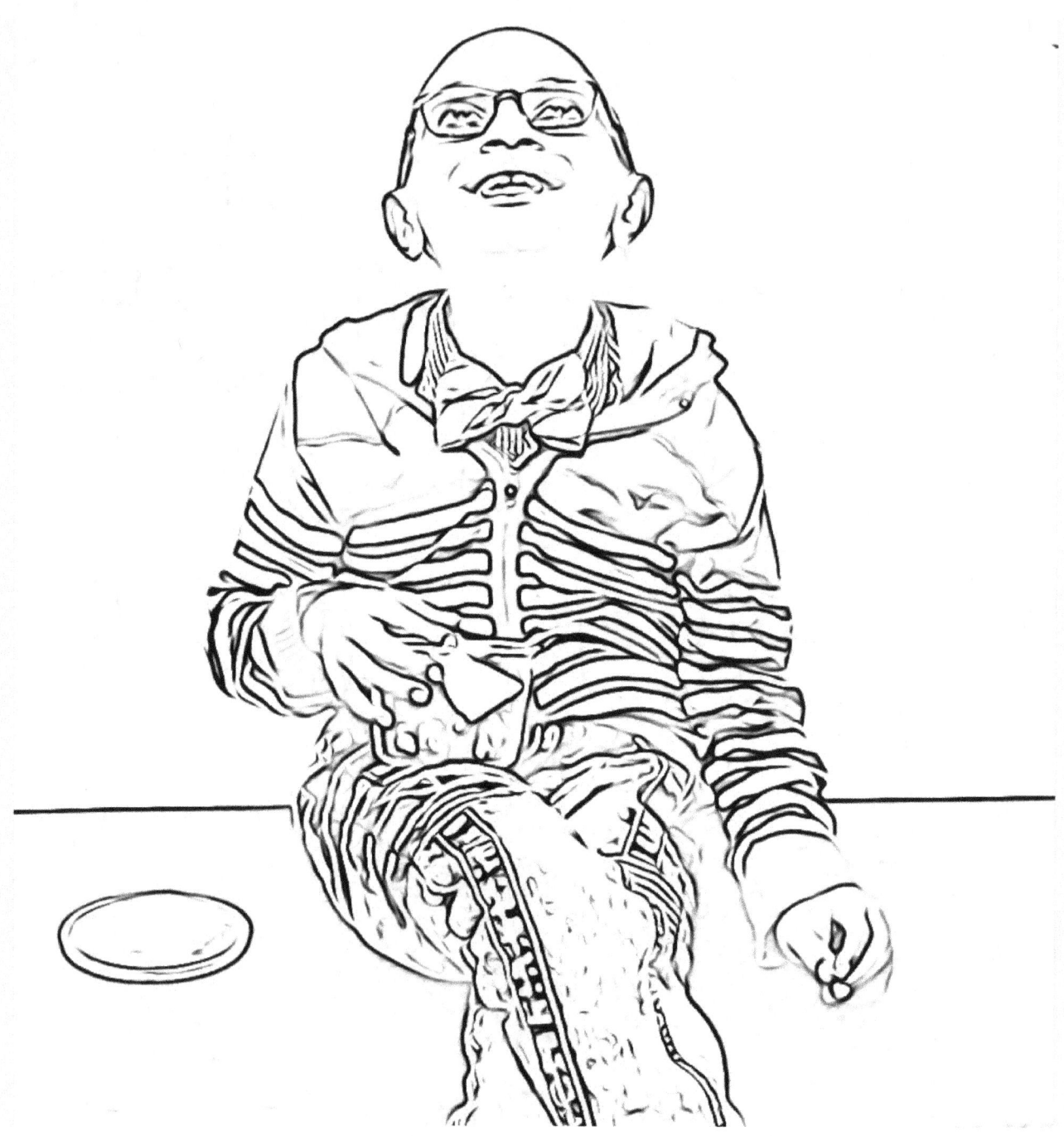

When love is expressed effectively the child learns how to see what's good about life (Looking Up) optimistically.

Coloring With Kindness, Page 24

Patient Love Is Kind
Richard Patterson III

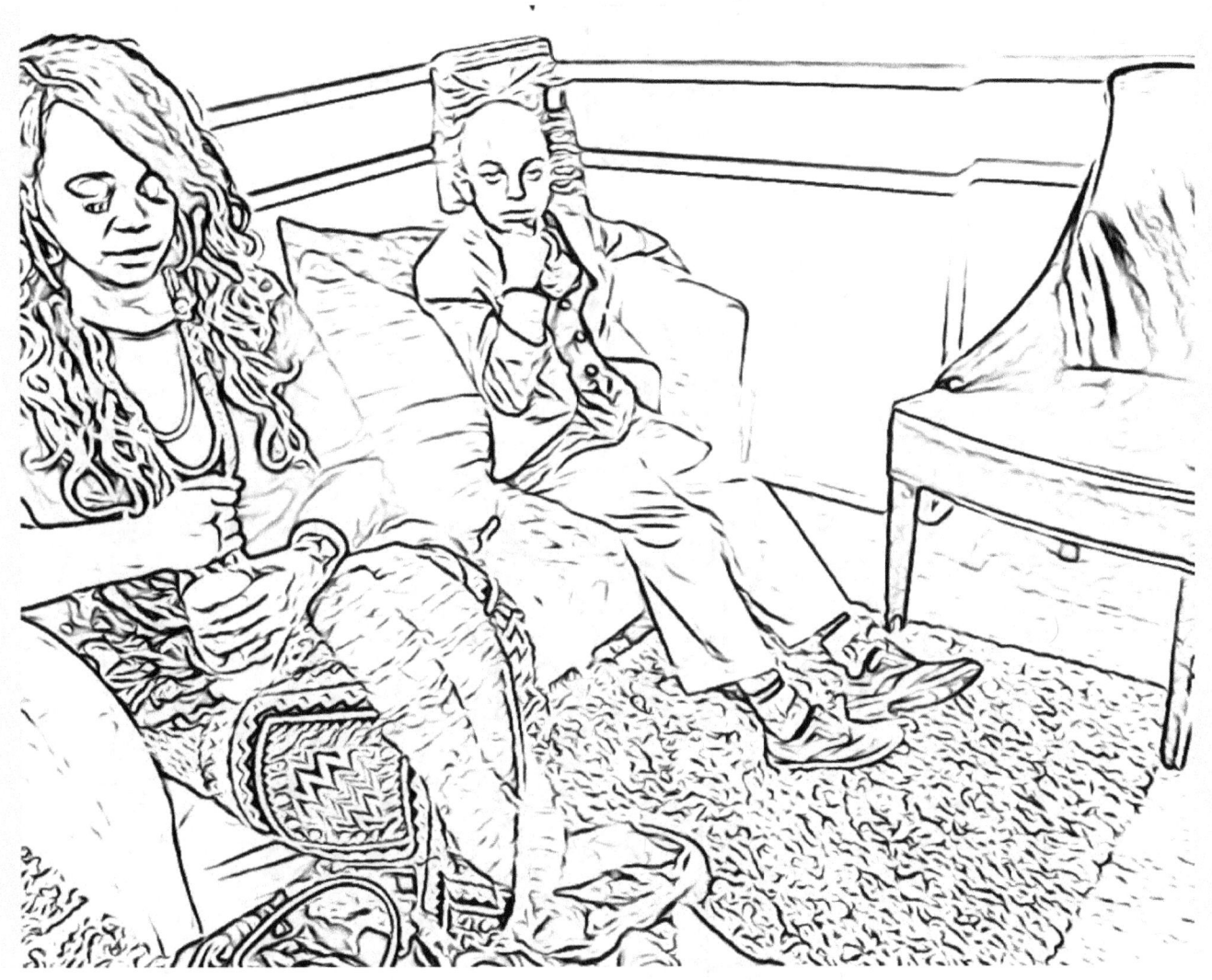

Someone is watching how you treat people from afar. Patience is in the hands of the family.

Coloring With Kindness, Page 25

Patient Love Is Kind
Richard Patterson III

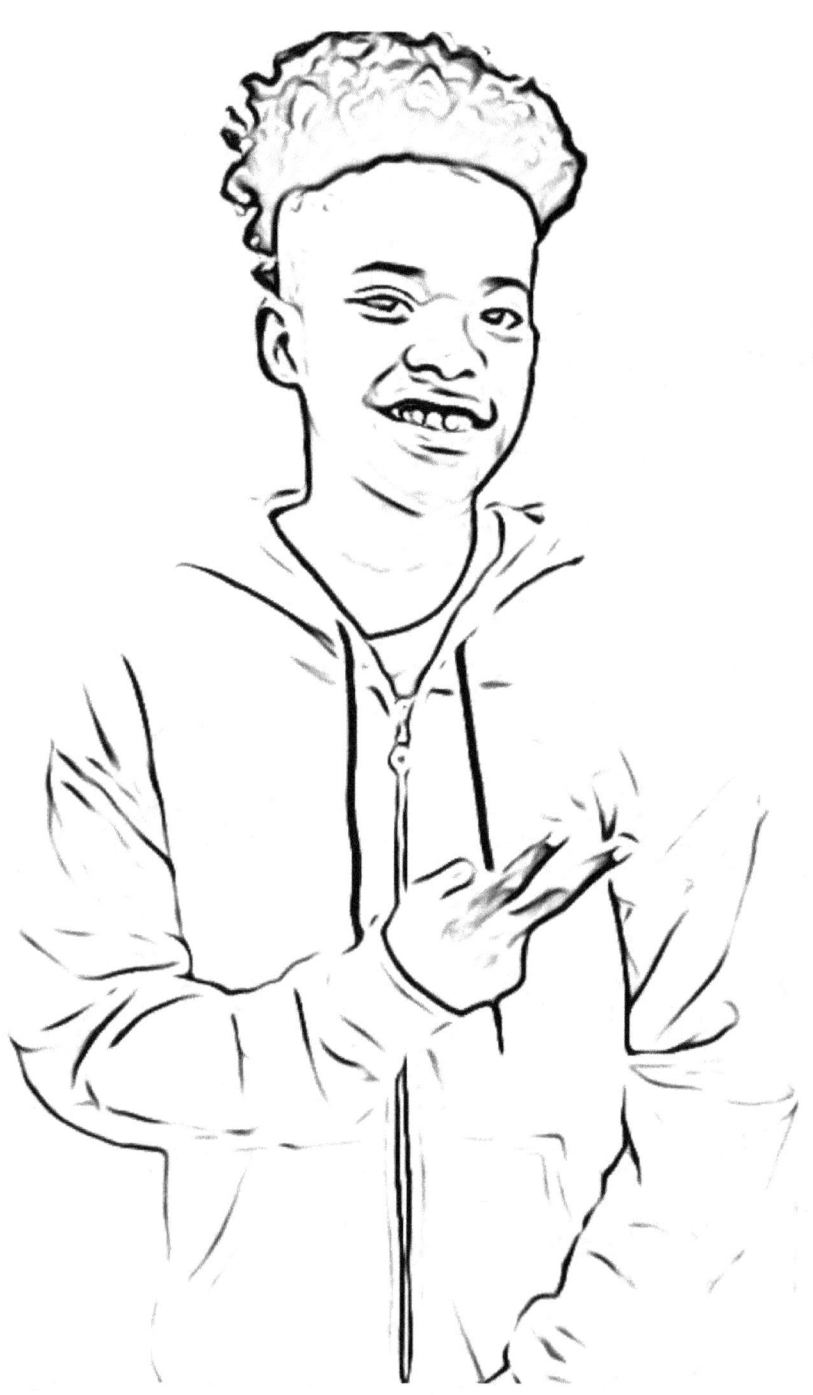

Love allows you to be seated comfortably, understanding you have the acceptance you need.

Patient Love Is Kind
Richard Patterson III

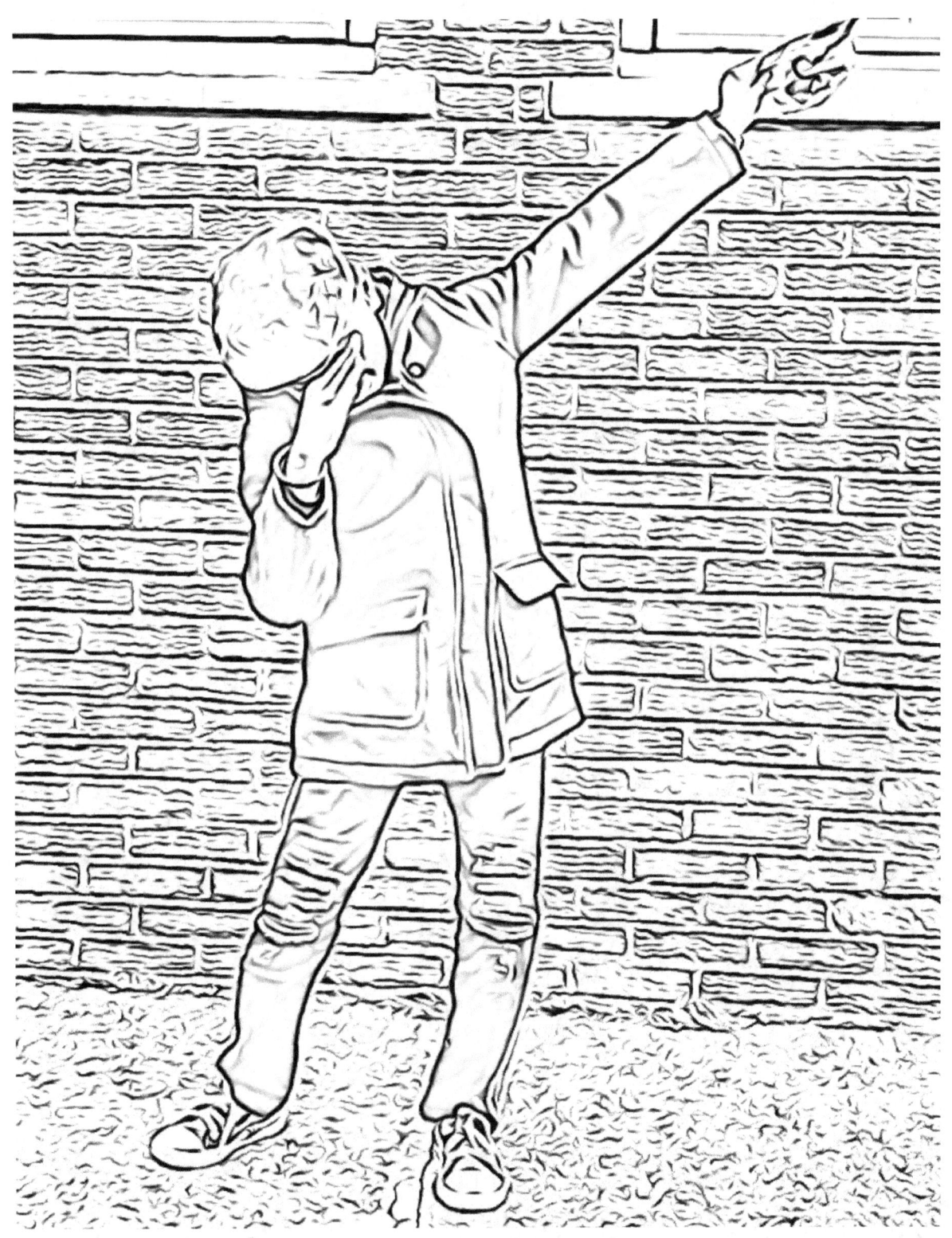

Love gives you the confidence to be you, even if that's being a bit animated.

Patient Love Is Kind
Richard Patterson III

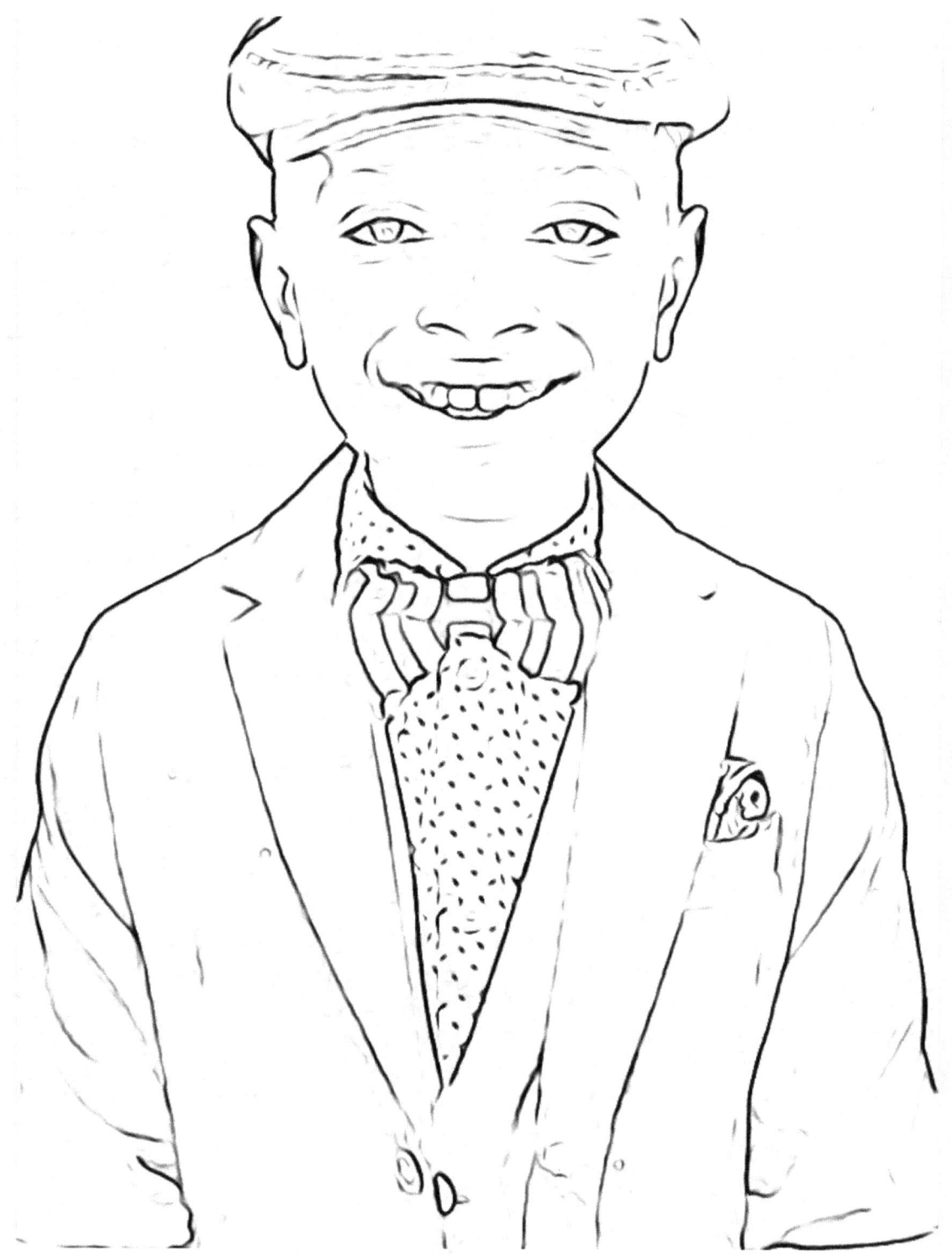

Love makes you smile for no reason. Love is how you live your best life and become the best version of yourself.

Coloring With Kindness, Page 28

Patient Love Is Kind
Richard Patterson III

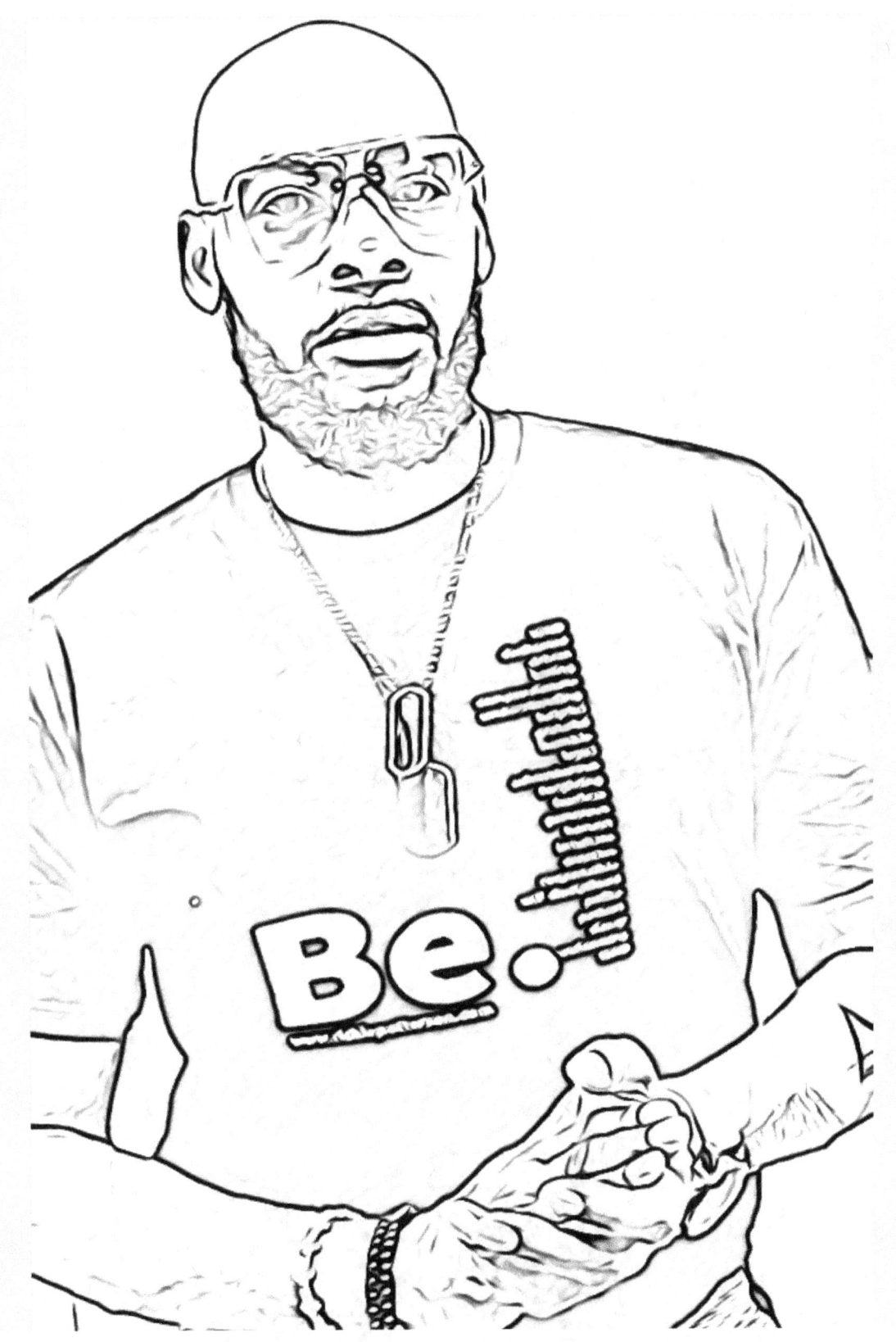

We are not who we are by accident, there are people who remind us to be Kind.

Coloring With Kindness, Page 29

Patient Love Is Kind
Richard Patterson III

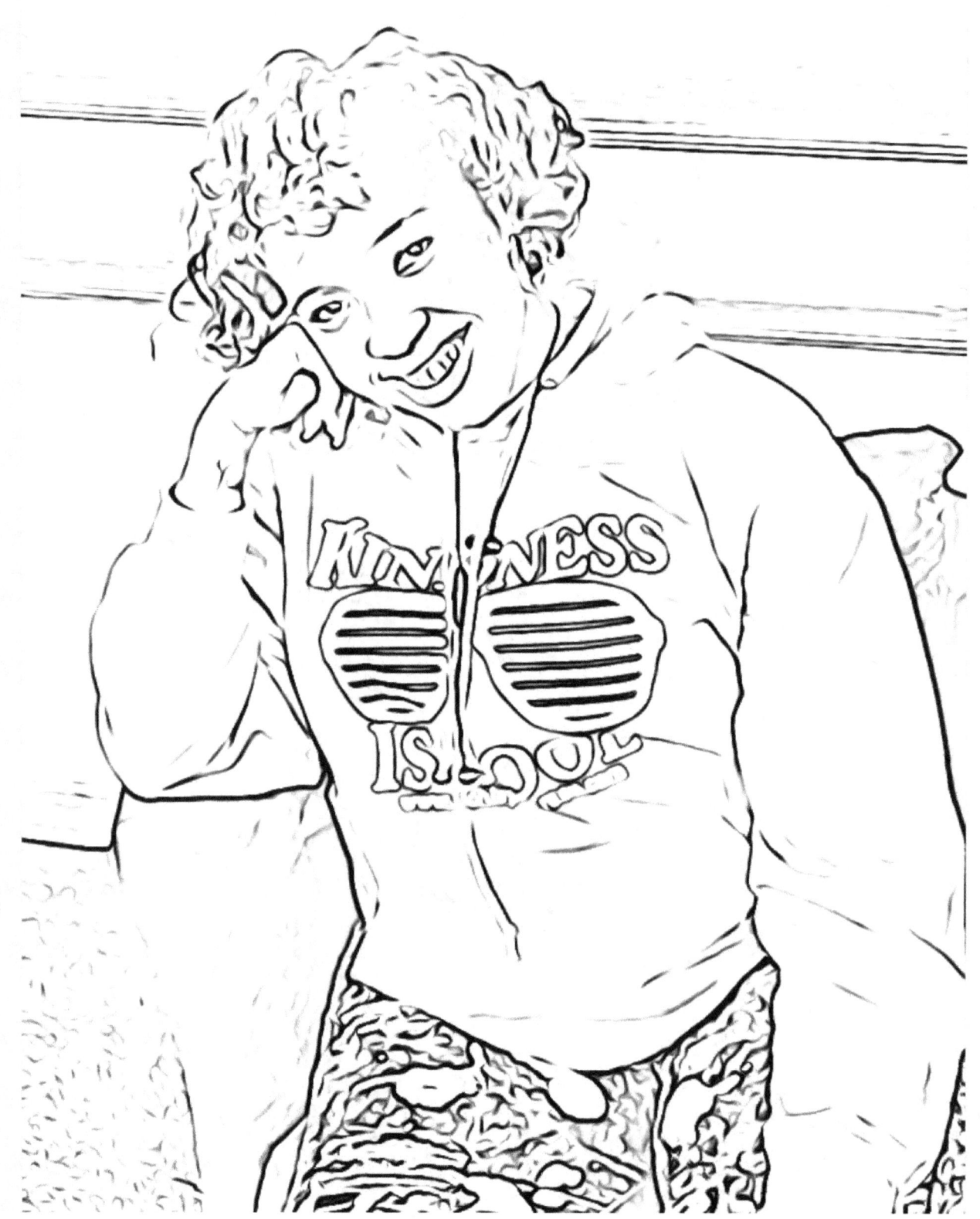

Love is patient and love is Kind.

Coloring With Kindness, Page 30

Patient Love Is Kind
Richard Patterson III

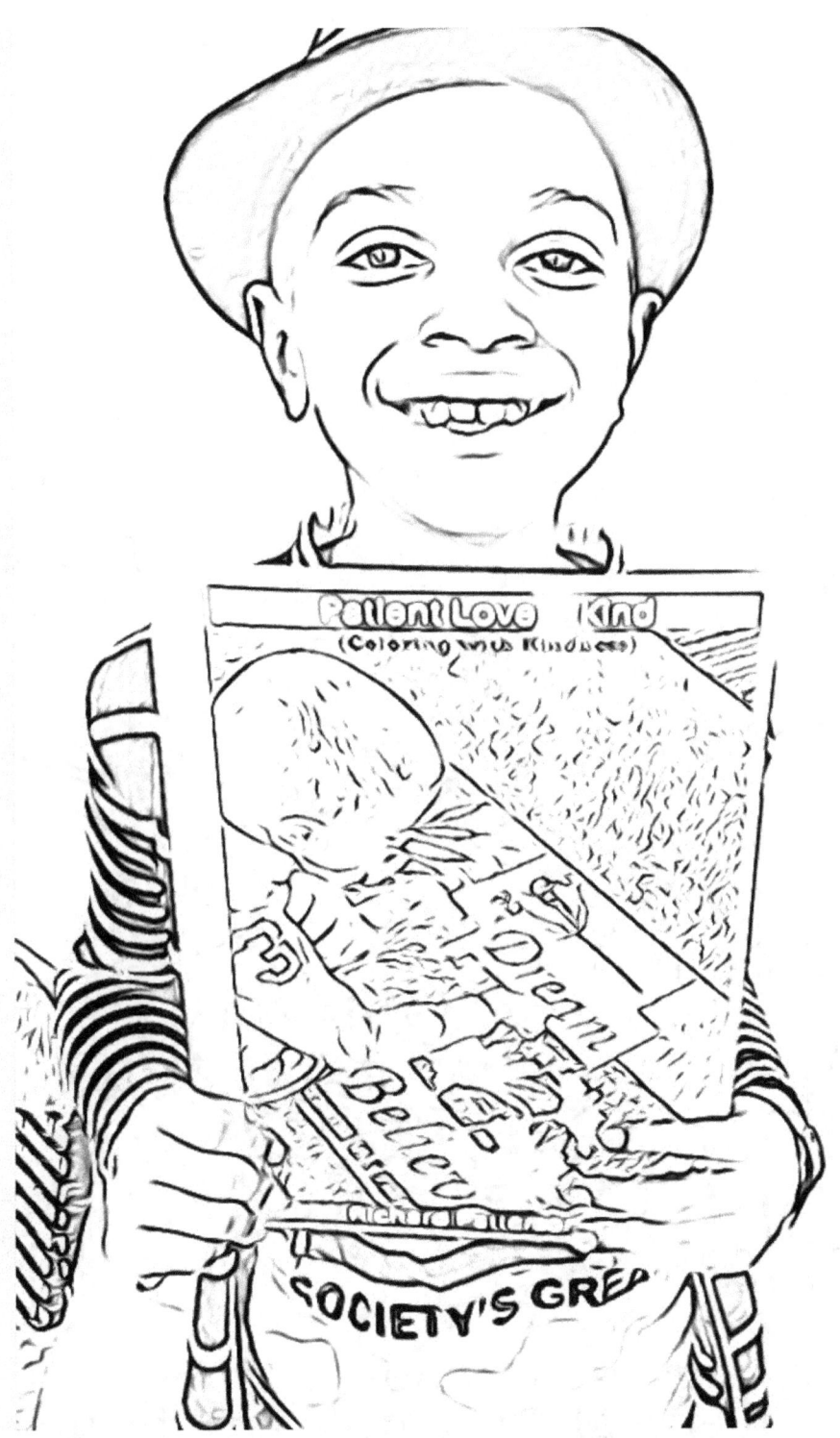

The patience you display in the lives of those you love will be the Kindness you reap as you age. Love reciprocates back when you need it most

Patient Love Is Kind
Richard Patterson III

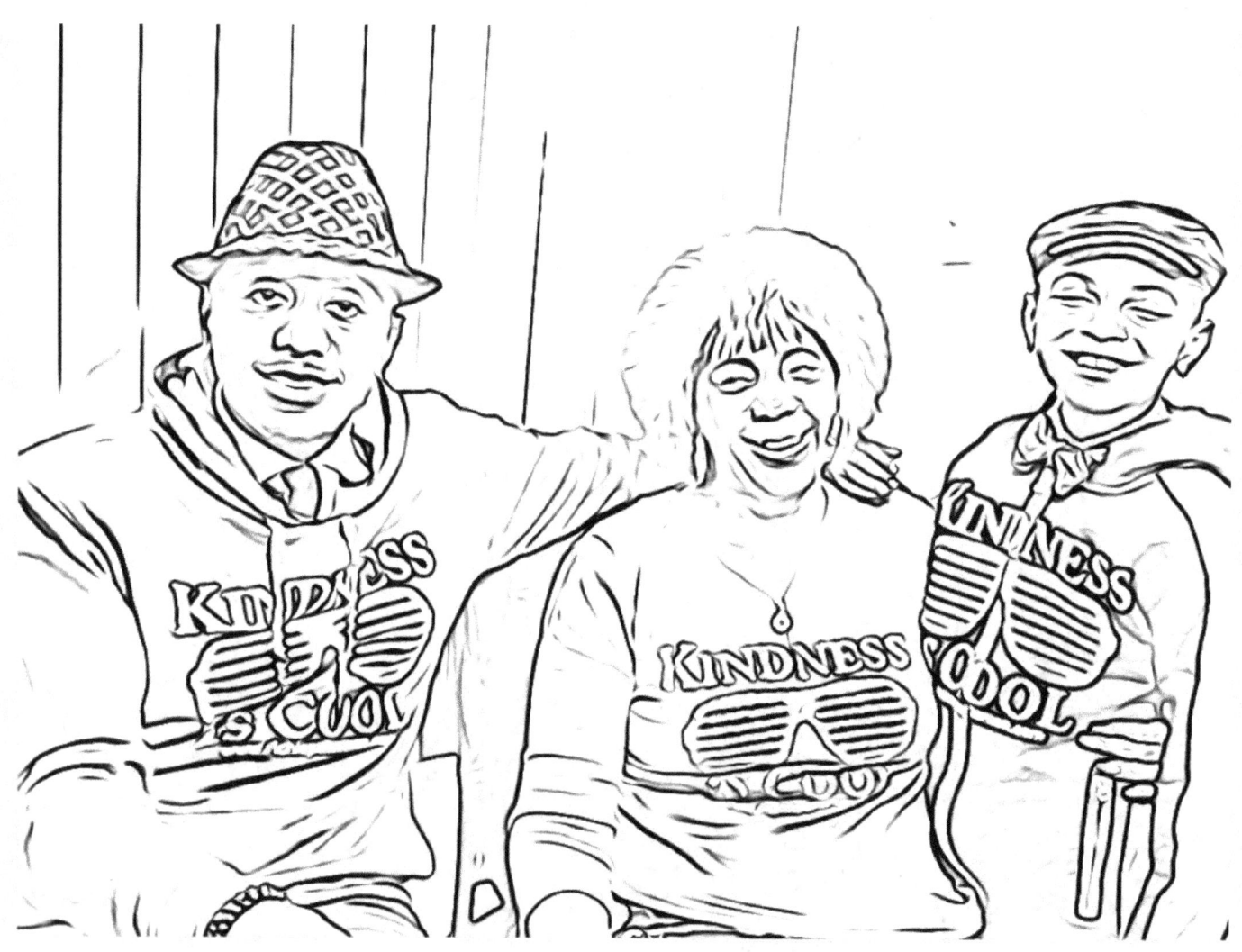

Whether you are generation Z, X, Baby Boomers or Millennial. Love creates a bridge for every generation to relate effectively.

Patient Love Is Kind
Richard Patterson III

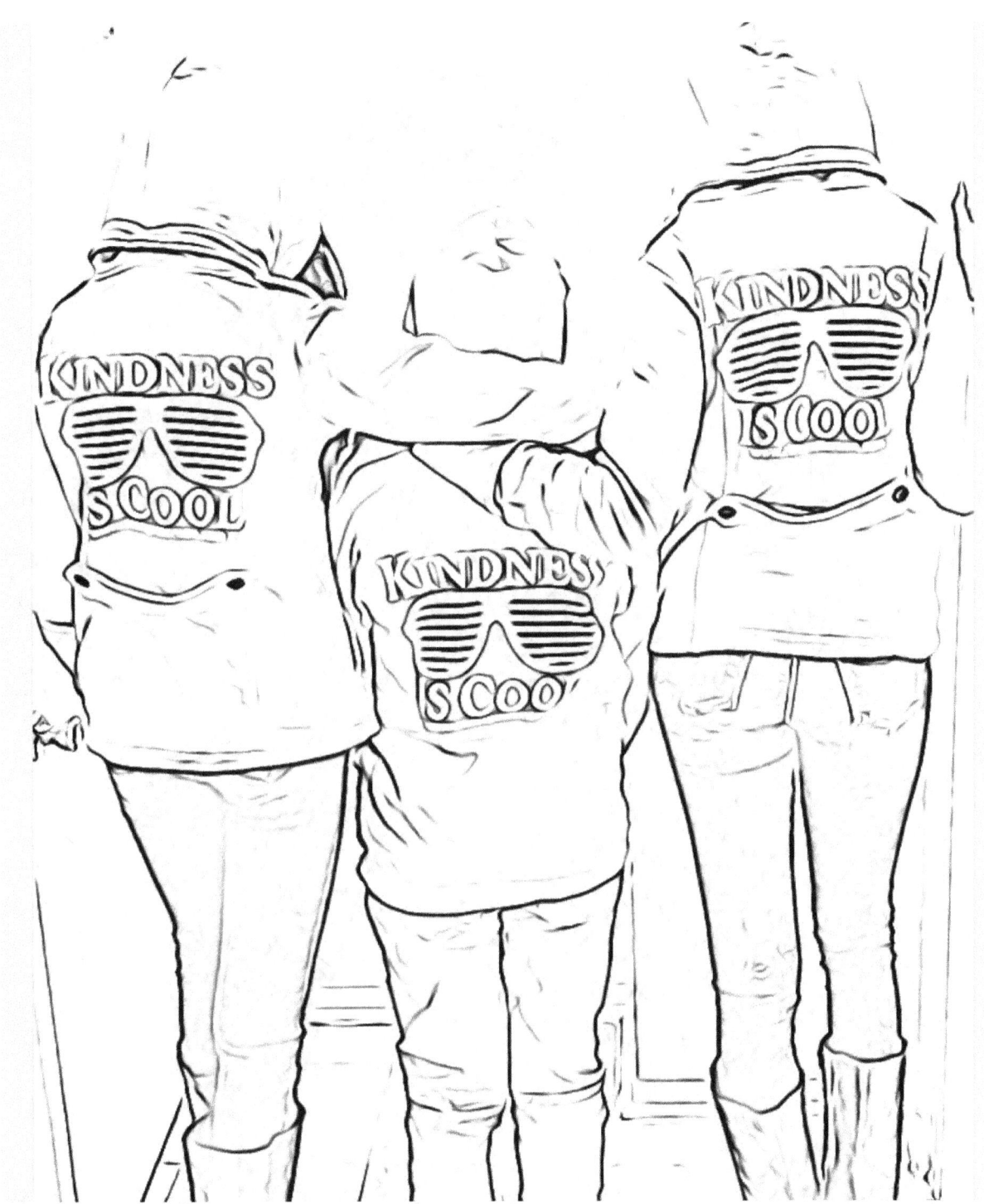

Love spends time and is patient enough to understand that your presence matters In relationships. That's the real Kindness

Patient Love Is Kind
Richard Patterson III

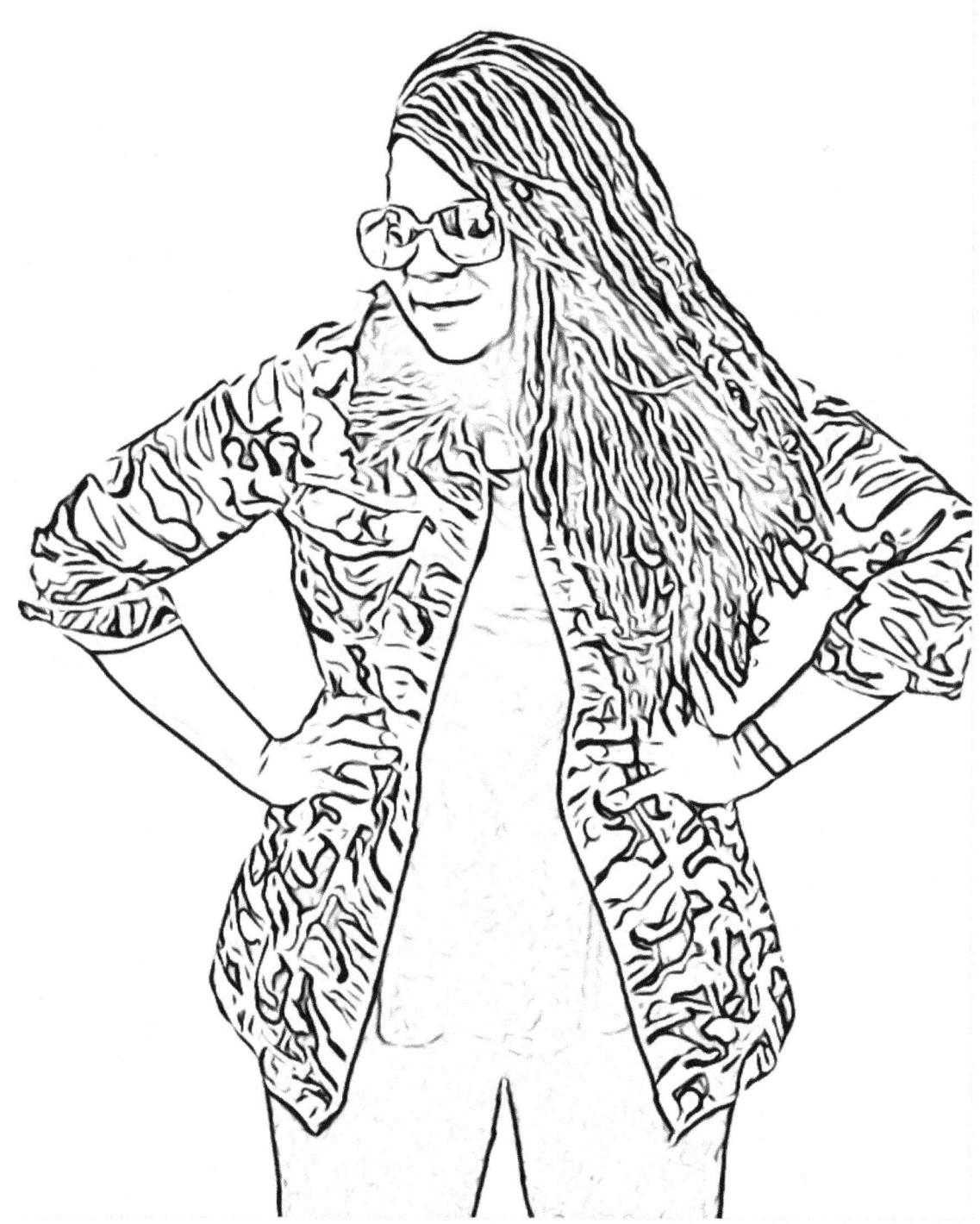

The next generation being patient, expressing love Through Kindness is as simple as showing them what love looks like through our example.

Patient Love Is Kind
Richard Patterson III

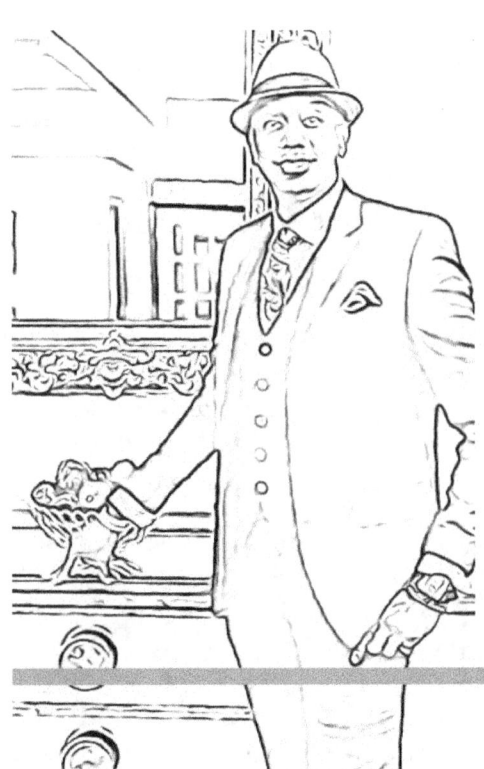

Available for Workshops, Speaking Engagements, Open Forums, Counseling Sessions And More

Pastor Richie Patterson III
8225 Allen Rd #1018
Allen Park, MI 48101
248.372.9500
www.richiepatterson.com

#THISISTHEKINDNESS
#COLORINGWITHKINDNESS

Patient Love Is Kind
Richard Patterson III

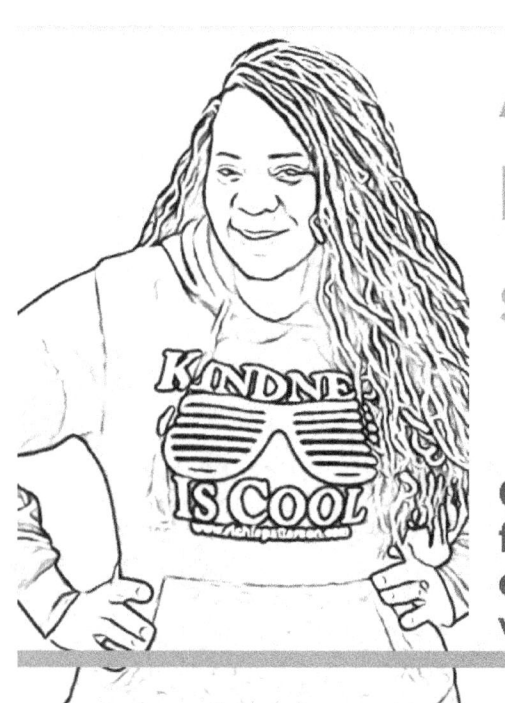

ADHD could not win because you showed up everyday

Cultivating creativity & family values through coloring
www.richiepatterson.com

#THISISTHEKINDNESS #COLORINGWITHKINDNESS

Patient Love Is Kind
Richard Patterson III

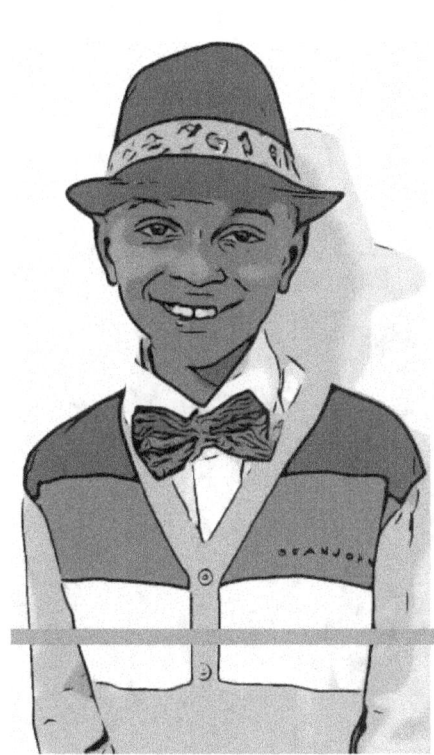

Developing focus and positive self esteem through Coloring

Cultivating Creativity through Coloring with Kindness
www.richiepatterson.com

#THISISTHEKINDNESS
#COLORINGWITHKINDNESS

Patient Love Is Kind
Richard Patterson III

Creating A Kind Culture

Kind Culture

www.richiepatterson.com

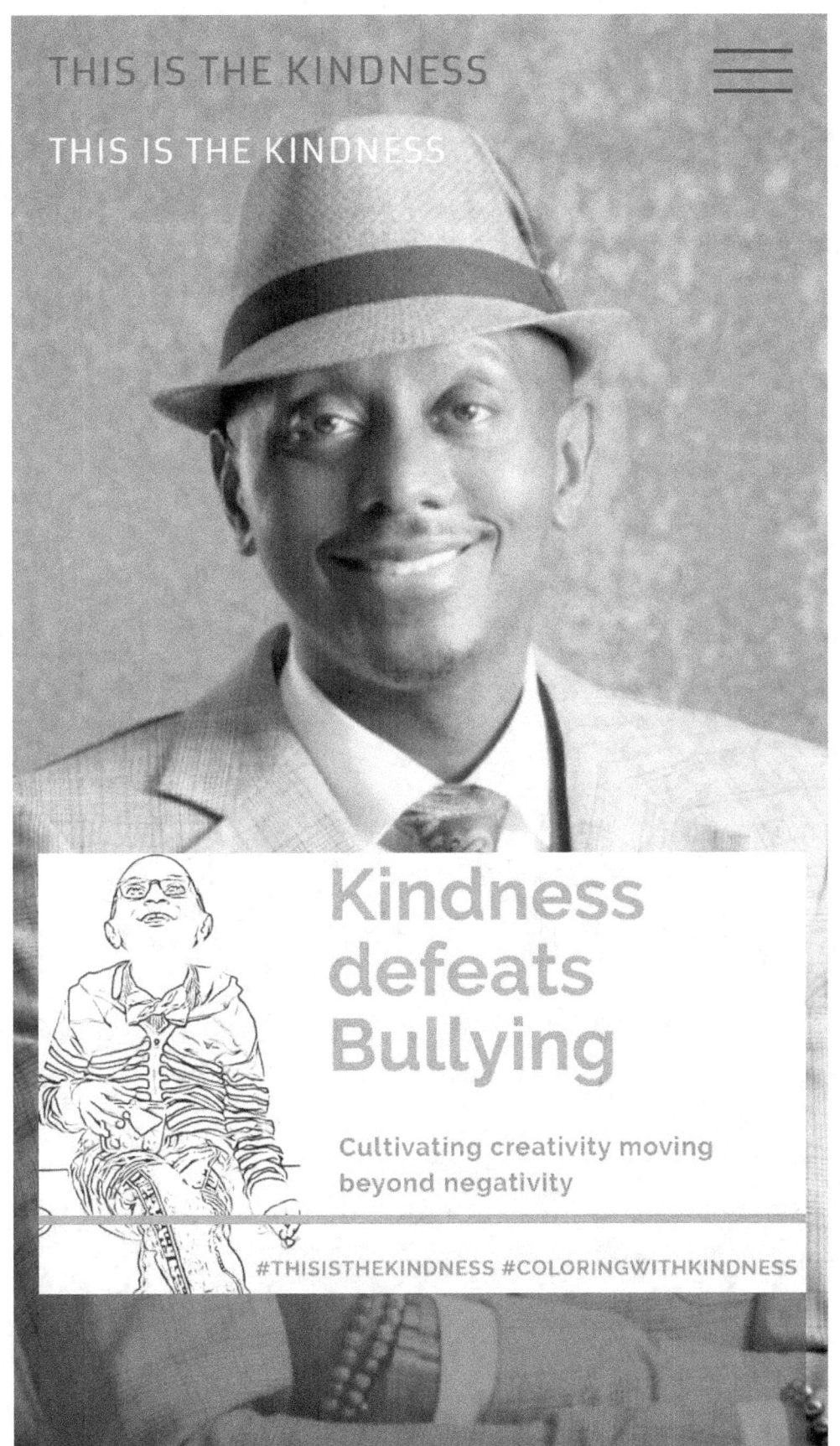

Patient Love Is Kind
Richard Patterson III

www.ingramcontent.com/pod-product-compliance
Lightning Source LLC
Chambersburg PA
CBHW062344220526
45469CB00008B/2835